SERVING
FACE

to perform at *Boyz* magazine's annual awards."

FELIX LE FREAK

SERVING
FACE

Lessons on Poise and (Dis)grace
from the World of Drag

FOREWORD BY **MONÉT X CHANGE**

A Note on Queer

"Queer" is a hotly debated word. It has been weaponized against LGBTQ+ people and for many is a hurtful slur. On the other hand, it's been used within the gay community for at least a century and has played a pivotal role in uniting LGBTQ+ people in art and activism. In this book, "queer" is a triumphant word, representing the celebration of difference and the power of LGBTQ+ people to overcome marginalization and flourish in the face of adversity. Queer also encompasses aesthetic sensibilities and systems of political resistance that cannot always be denoted by an inexhaustive acronym. If you aren't comfortable with the word queer, feel free to mentally substitute it with whichever descriptor makes you feel most fabulous.

A Note on Pronouns

The artists featured within this book are referred to either by the preferred pronoun of their drag persona or, in a minority of cases, that of the artist themselves. This may bring about one or two amusing idiosyncrasies (for example, "I'm a hairy man," she says), but such is the fun of drag. Just go with it.

CONTENTS

FOREWORD

This year marks my eighth anniversary as a drag queen, and interview after interview, I am often asked, "What is drag?" People are obsessed with compressing the intricate history of drag into a cute little sound bite or a few perfectly worded sentences for their blogs or publications. This may work for some, but as long as we are focusing on *what is drag*, we are forgetting *who is drag*, and that is the beauty of *Serving Face*.

Growing up as a little gay boy in New York City, I remember riding the subway to school and occasionally seeing these beautiful nightlife creatures retiring home after a night of blissful debauchery, and I would be absolutely stunned. Thirteen-year-old me would sit in awe of their unabashed rapture, and how they entranced an entire train station full of early morning commuters with a loud and boisterous, "Good morning!" I didn't know it then, but from these frivolous interactions, I was gaining profound cognition. I was learning confidence. I was learning courage. I was learning how to simultaneously throw up in your purse and count your tips from the night before—a talent I've had to call on more times than I care to admit. Though these experiences bring light to just one facet of *who* drag is, they represent an important piece of the fabric that drag weaves.

I've personally had the displeasure of working with many of the artists that are mentioned in this book, and I'm immediately reminded of the symbiosis of drag, a very real and palatable energy. As much as you will learn about the beauty, resilience, and politics of drag, you will discover how queens also learn from each other. Well, most of us—Peaches Christ tends to "march to the beat of her own drum," and that's very evident if you find yourself staring at her face in the front row of The Castro Theater.

Without the giants from yesterday, it would be next to impossible for the legends of tomorrow to arise. We've heard enough about those silly girls from that one TV show. The stories echoed throughout this book about the *who's* of drag from around the world are the stories that need to be told.

Monét x

Monét X Change, captured by Steven Simione in Jersey City, New York, May 2020.

WELCOME TO SERVING FACE

The library is officially open, dear reader.

Unless you've been living under a rock, you may have noticed that drag is having a moment. Once coyly concealed under the cloak of night, only rearing its impeccably coiffed head in occasional pantomimes and carnivals, drag has since strutted out of the gay bar into the mainstream, creating household names and leaving brand-new industries in its wake. Drag is on our televisions; in our music; hosting our brunches; and, before long, it will be bursting forth from our morning cereal in a shower of confetti. Drag is a bona fide cultural phenomenon, honey.

I, myself, fell into drag by virtue of chaos, upheaval, and happenstance. A graduate of two delightful but useless theater degrees and a PhD in disappointment from the University of Life, I found myself locked out of the mainstream arts and pushed deeper and deeper into desk-bound drudgery. One night in 2016, in a fit of laudanum-induced despair, I sent off an application form for an amateur drag competition in London. Against the odds, I was invited to compete the following week.

It would be disingenuous to suggest that I knew nothing of drag. I wrote my undergraduate dissertation on the topic, exploring the use of clothing as costume in the performance of gender from the 19th century through to the present day. But I knew very little about how to actually *do* it. In a frenzy, I ordered a mesh leotard and clip-in ponytail, dug out a children's face painting kit that had been gathering dust, and hoped for the best.

What I discovered on my first night at the now-defunct Her Upstairs in Camden Town was a diverse community of queer creatives, brimming with weirdness and excellence. I fell in love with the London cabaret scene immediately. There was dance, burlesque, music, parody, buckets of fake blood, and even inflatable accordions. I wasn't sure what it all meant, but I knew that my aching gay heart, drained by the confines of normality and artistic displacement, was starting to beat again. I can only hope the eclectic array of artistry within this volume can do a fraction of that for you, dear reader.

Within a year, I had quit my job and entered every competition going, winning a few, including the largest queer talent contest in the country, *Drag Idol UK* (2018), with a combination of creative performance art pieces and original musical comedy sets. In these past few short years, I've been blessed with countless opportunities, traveled the world, enjoyed several celebrity affairs (one royal), and even had a cruise liner named after me (thank you, your highness). To top it all off, someone has now seen fit to make me an author. If you're reading this, then I'm thrilled to announce I was not required to return my advance.

Serving Face is my love letter to the ingenuity, diversity, and creative excellence of queer LGBTQ+ performance art. The incredible artists contained within these pages have been lovingly selected in order to showcase a glittering spectrum of contemporary drag. No single one of them can tell you definitively what it means to be a king, queen, or a drag-in-between, because each artist's perspective is as unique as your own.

Some of our dear contributors are men and others are women. Some of them are cisgender (they identify with the gender they were assigned at birth), while others are trans (they do not). Others still are nonbinary (they do not identify as exclusively male or female). Some of these people are comedians, some are dancers, and others are visual artists. They span continents and cliques, but they have all been noted within their communities, or by the world, for the creative contribution they have made toward the art of drag.

These interviews cover a broad range of topics, from queer history and underground movements to the peaks and perils of the reality TV zeitgeist. What they have in common is a wealth of overflowing insight on life, style, and performance, straight from the unicorn's mouth!

This book is for everyone. Whether it is by deepening your understanding of queer and minority art forms or by encouraging you to try a bold new makeup look, I hope the wisdom of the artists featured here brings you inspiration and enjoyment, and perhaps even puts an extra skip in your strut.

Yours disgracefully,

Felix Le Freak

x

WHAT IS DRAG?

One might as soon ask, "How long is a piece of tucking tape?" because the question is something of a head scratcher. The pursuit of a definition has destroyed friendships, snatched wigs, befuddled academics, and revoked liquor licenses. The truth is that nobody seems quite sure.

The disagreements begin with the origin of the term. There are those who declare loudly from overdrawn lips that it refers to long skirts "dragging" along the theater floor, while others throw down their purses in disdain at this claim and insist the term is an acronym for "dressed as a girl"—which sort of works, if you squint a bit.

A lesser-known theory supposes that the term has its origins in a slur for effeminate gay soldiers who would "drag" behind formation to chatter and fornicate. We can't possibly know if there is any truth to this, but we can dare to imagine that the gossip was juiciest at the rear.

Like art, drag evades definition. Art cannot be exhaustively summarized as oil on canvas, but we generally accept that an earthworm, or a Tuesday, is not art. Similarly, we cannot define drag exclusively as somebody "dressed as a girl," but we can assume that the New York Stock Exchange is probably not drag. At least we hope not.

What does exist is a canon of sorts: a series of references, motifs, and traditions woven together in large part by queer history and gender-nonconformity. Common themes are queer self-expression, the subversion of societally acceptable gender norms, and parody of the heteronormative (straight) world.

Drag's potential applications are no less varied. A person may call upon the magic of drag to create a comic portrayal of "the opposite sex", they may utilize drag to manifest a stylized version of their most authentic self; or they may use drag to reject binary gender altogether. Any gender can participate *in* drag, and any gender can be performed *as* drag. Drag can refer to the costume worn for a performance or to a performance itself. The possibilities are endless and counting.

It is worth noting that gay men dominate the written history of drag, but to define drag simply as men dressing in feminine attire would be a brutal injustice to the art and its myriad participants. Cisgender men are central to most written history, and the world of drag is no exception. Patriarchy, it seems, pervades even queer subculture.

Furthermore, trans and nonbinary artists have been founders in creating the language, aesthetic, and social structures of the drag style popular in today's mainstream. Much of the lingo made famous by *RuPaul's Drag Race* owes a debt to the ballroom scene, and trans kings and queens are still major players in the landscape of drag, despite being underrepresented on our TV screens.

So what is drag? For the sake of argument, I humbly proffer the following: Drag is a form of creative self-expression that uses costume, makeup, and/or performance to play with traditional notions of gender. Where society has said, "This is a man and this is a woman," drag has stuck out its tongue and brazenly answered, "No!"

However you prefer to define it, people have been slipping into each other's panties and making a scene since time immemorial. We have no way of knowing who first donned the "wrong" loincloth. All we can do is pinpoint a few of the sparkling peaks and embarrassing stumbles in history and wonder with bated breath where drag is going next. I, for one, am on tenterhooks.

THE EVOLUTION OF DRAG
WHERE IT BEGAN

Queer culture has long been tied to the history of the theater. In Shakespeare's London, women were not permitted on stage, so men wore female attire to play female roles, and we can imagine that many of these performances were delivered with a knowing flourish and flair. However, female impersonation existed here as a specialist skill that evolved in response to the cultural exclusion of women. It was a practical subversion rather than a deliberate political transgression.

Women finally made it onto the European stage in the 17th century, and by the 18th century, female sopranos were frequently cast in "breeches roles" as adolescent boys in Italian operas. By this time, the majority of men who played female roles did so for comic relief. The tropes of the lead boy and pantomime dame have persisted to the present day.

Beneath the veneer of popular entertainment were the Molly houses of 18th-century England, illicit meeting places for gay men where "cross-dressing" was rife and mock weddings—and even births—were performed. Though often raided, arrested, and persecuted, the homosexuals and "effeminates" would continue to meet in such a manner well into the Victorian period.

Meanwhile, in the US, the first person to describe themselves as a "queen of drag" appears to be African-American William Dorsey Swann, a former slave and gay liberation activist. Swann threw elaborate drag balls for black queers in 1880s Washington, DC and campaigned for the right of his community to gather without persecution. His soirées are arguably the origin of the modern "ballroom" scene.

Female impersonation as commercial entertainment saw a boom in the vaudeville tradition of the late 19th and early 20th centuries, making a particular star of American actor Julian Etlinge. However, negative associations with homosexuality and sex work led to the decline of the tradition during the anti-corruption crackdowns of the Progressive Era. Drag would later resurface as an underground art form during the Prohibition Era, a phenomenon known as the Pansy Craze.

By the early to mid-20th century, drag was almost exclusively associated with gay nightlife culture, and, therefore, criminal deviancy. Under the cover of darkness, in houses of ill repute on the wrong sides of the wrong towns, queer people met to express themselves and challenge the boundaries of gender. It was here that modern drag started to take shape.

DRAG IN THE AGE OF CIVIL LIBERTY

In the second half of the 20th century, drag became intertwined with activism and counterculture. Central to the Stonewall riots of 1969 were Sylvia Rivera and Marsha P. Johnson, two self-described drag queens who went on to found the Street Transvestite Action Revolutionaries, a group dedicated to helping homeless queer youth. While the exact language was not available at the time, Rivera and Johnson are widely understood to have been trans women.

In the 1970s, gay filmmaker John Waters directed transgressive cult movies that offended polite sensibilities and made a star out of drag queen Divine. As Babs Johnson in *Pink Flamingos* (1972), Divine famously declared, "Kill everyone now. Condone first-degree murder. Advocate cannibalism. Eat shit. Filth are my politics. Filth is my life"—a monologue which cemented her as an icon of anti-establishment drag.

Throughout this era, drag was also making a return to more polite circles. In the 1960s, Irish singer and female impersonator Danny LaRue was among Britain's highest-paid entertainers, wowing audiences on the West End with his impressions of gay icons, including Elizabeth Taylor, Judy Garland, and Zsa Zsa Gabor.

Following on from the sexual liberation of the 1960s and the psychedelic, gender-bending of performance groups, such as The Cockettes, pop music made androgyny cool to the masses. In glam rock, punk, and later new wave, gender-defying fashion became the rage, while *The Rocky Horror Picture Show* (1975) became a cult hit among queer and nonqueer audiences alike.

The 1980s saw the rise of flamboyant pop stars, such as Boy George and Pete Burns, as well as the birth of the club kids, outrageous New York City nightclub personalities known for their wild parties and avant-garde looks.

In 1990, the documentary film *Paris Is Burning* chronicled the Harlem ballroom scene, in which black and Latinx drag queens and trans performers formed "houses" as surrogate families and competed for titles in various pageant-style categories. In the same year, the associated dance style known as "vogueing" gained popular attention as the subject of a Madonna single and music video. The ballroom scene was more recently dramatized in the HBO series *Pose*.

Drag remained a popular niche within both the queer community and working-class variety cabaret throughout the 1990s and 2000s, but it appeared in the mainstream predominantly as a novelty or the butt of the joke. Character comics like Dame Edna and Lily Savage dominated primetime chat shows. Popular movies, such as *The Adventures of Priscilla, Queen of the Desert* (1994); *Too Wong Foo, Thanks for Everything, Julie Newmar* (1995); and *The Birdcage* (1996) featured lovable characters but ultimately portrayed drag as odd, dated, and anything but cool.

THE GREAT DRAG GLOW UP

Everything changed in the late 2000s with the debut of *RuPaul's Drag Race*, a satirical twist on reality television talent contests. It featured a cast comprised mainly of gay men performing various challenges in female drag in the hopes of becoming America's Next Drag Superstar. The show was an enormous viral hit, winning awards, franchising internationally, and inspiring an entire generation of young LGBTQ+ people to pick up a makeup brush and utilize the once-dated tradition to express themselves in new and exciting ways.

Around the same time, Lady Gaga followed in Madonna's footsteps by putting queer culture and aesthetics front and center. She dressed like a drag queen, wore brightly colored lace-front wigs, and sang lyrics celebrating the LGBTQ+ community. In doing so, she also spawned thousands of drag tributes worldwide, giving female impersonators an excuse to wear lobsters on their heads.

The role of social media cannot be understated in the boom that came next. Where once a fledgling queen would need to seek out niche spaces to learn the art of drag, suddenly there was viral reality TV showcasing it, YouTube tutorials teaching it, and online communities of like-minded people bonding over it.

Streaming culture and social media not only made drag cool, they made it accessible. This led to rapid developments in the art of drag makeup. Beauty bloggers and makeup gurus amassed millions of followers for their channels demonstrating drag techniques. Mainstream celebrities shared their contouring routines. Where once the idea that a woman might "look like a drag queen" was thrown down as a pejorative, in the 2010s, drag became a primary influencer in the multi-billion-dollar cosmetics industry.

At the same time, live venues in cities around the world experienced an unprecedented drag renaissance. Pageants, revues, club nights, and amateur competitions sprang up in bars and nightclubs, and a new cohort of queer talent began to emerge. Which brings us to …

ONWARD AND UPWARD

The new drag quickly became an artistic haven for countless queer performers. While LGBTQ+ actors, dancers, and musicians are plentiful, they often struggle for exposure within mainstream arts, where queer people rarely headline commercial products. Of the top 10 grossing LGBTQ+ themed films released over the past two decades, no openly LGBTQ+ actor has featured in a lead role, while heterosexual actors are often piled high with awards and gushing praise for "going gay."

With access limited in traditional forms, a wave of queer talent now appears to be migrating to drag, an industry where individuals can not only survive, but thrive by means of expressing themselves authentically. Ironically, drag's runaway success is beginning to make it a hot property among more conventional audiences, so the mainstream finds itself chasing drag's divine coattails in search of a lucrative slice of its glee and innovation. We can only hope this has a lasting, positive impact for queer visibility and opportunity.

The future of drag is ablaze with possibility. Contemporary drag is not limited to one style or one medium. The artists of today range from cunning gender-illusionists to outright gender rebels. For every bejeweled songstress in a jazz bar, there is a high-kicking, death-dropping dynamo on a dance floor down the street. The lineup of any one drag show might contain a crooning king and an ethereal entity performing stunning live art outside the bounds of gender altogether.

Drag can be all about the makeup, as shown by the stars of social media, or it can be all about performance, as seen in the clubs and cabarets. It can employ the art of lip-sync to tell complex, beautiful, and hilarious stories, or it can be a platform for a live singer to belt out a show tune they would never get the chance to sing on Broadway. Drag can be silly or serious. It can be URL or IRL. Drag can be anything it wants to be.

As its popularity continues to rise and drag becomes increasingly detached from the communities that birthed it, the challenge for emerging artists will be in learning its history; understanding its cultural importance; and respecting not only its ability, but its responsibility to make positive change.

Drag is important, not just for the LGBTQ+ community, but for everyone. Drag shows us that it's okay to make ourselves larger, to throw off conformity and fantasize our wildest selves. It teaches us to make noise and take up space. In a world bogged down by humdrum conformity, divisive politics, and rank inequality, drag wielded correctly is a tool of revolution.

A word of advice: The best way to experience drag is to get out into the community and see it for yourself. This book hopes to visit as many corners of the scene as possible, but it is only by supporting your local drag artists that you can hope to discover the ways in which people are sharing their art in its newest and rawest forms. If you don't have a local scene, why not start one? If you can't get out, get online and see what people are creating there.

In the words of Mother Ru, good luck, and don't fuck it up.

GLOSSARY OF TERMS

AFAB Assigned female at birth (preferred to "biologically female" or "born as a girl").

AMAB Assigned male at birth (preferred to "biologically male" or "born as a boy").

Ballroom An underground black and Latinx LGBTQ+ subculture.

Beat Makeup or the application of makeup–for example, "Check out her fierce beat!"

Bind To flatten and conceal the bust and create a flat surface.

Cabaret An informal performance venue, show, or style of entertainment, often in a bar.

Camp Having a whimsical, mischievous quality, particularly associated with LGBTQ+ people.

Cinch To pull in one's waistline using a corset.

Cis/Cisgender Identifying with the gender one was assigned at birth–in other words, not trans.

Clock To recognize a "fault" in someone's appearance, such as stubble showing through.

Contour Darker foundation used to create depth and shadow.

Cut crease A shape drawn above the eye to create a larger, false eyelid shape.

Drag Artist An artist exploring gender.

Drag King An artist exploring masculinity.

Drag Queen An artist exploring femininity.

For the gods Done extremely well.

Gag An expression of pleasant shock and awe.

Genderqueer Not subscribing to traditional gender distinctions.

Gender illusionist An artist whose aesthetic focus is the embodiment of any gender other than their own.

Heteronormative Denoting a worldview that presumes heterosexuality as the default.

Highlight Lighter foundation used to bring areas of the face forward.

Lace front A professional wig with a realistic hairline.

LGBTQ+ Lesbian, gay, bisexual, trans, queer, and other minority gender and sexual identities.

Look An entire ensemble including makeup, hair, and costume.

Mug One's face or the makeup design painted on it.

Nonbinary Identifying neither exclusively male nor exclusively female.

Pad To flesh out body parts such as the hips using foam.

Paint To apply makeup.

Patriarchy A system or society in which men hold the majority of power.

Queer An umbrella term for sexual and gender minorities, as well as the art, literature, and politics that reflect the sensibilities of LGBTQ+ people.

Read To sharply analyze or criticize.

Realness Authenticity in any desired look, particularly full gender illusion.

Serve To deliver to an audience.

Shade Disrespect.

Sickening Jaw-droppingly good.

Slay To perform exceedingly well.

Snatched Flawlessly made up.

Tea Gossip.

Trans Not identifying with the gender one was assigned at birth.

Tuck To flatten and conceal the crotch and create a flat surface.

Dapper Chaps and

CAMP

Bawdy Broads

From laugh-a-minute cabaret queens to suited and booted killer kings, these entertainers embody humor, theatricality, and a pointedly tongue-in-cheek take on gender. Camp is all about holding up a mirror to the traditional world and beaming back its image through a lens of exaggeration and whimsy.

STEPPING UP TO THE MIC WITH

MISS COCO PERU

Bona-fide queer legend Miss Coco Peru has been performing in drag for three decades. She rose to prominence in the early '90s as a downtown favorite in New York City with her one-woman cabaret shows and has since gone on to star in countless TV shows and movies. Here, she discusses her early influences, signature style, and why your dreams should always be bigger than your fears.

"Taken by Peter Palladino in the Camelot Movie Theater. I had asked Peter if he could take a few photos of me before my show that evening, and we both saw the hideous mural and thought, 'Perfect!'"

"I count my first introduction to drag as a puppet," says Coco. "It was Wayland Flowers and Madame. Madame was the puppet, and I was very young, but I somehow made the connection that this puppet was given a voice by a gay man. She was over the top, fabulous, and raunchy, and I loved the sense of humor. Later in life, I realized Madame was almost a version of drag. It's obvious now why it resonated with me so much."

When she finally came out as gay, Coco visited a bar called The Monster in New York City, where she saw her first drag queen in the flesh. "Downstairs they had a tiny stage," she remembers, "and there was a black drag queen doing 'Goldfinger' by Shirley Bassey. I was fascinated because I'd never seen anything quite like that."

The show that finally inspired Coco's cabaret persona was The Lady in Question is Charles Busch. "Charles Busch played the female lead," she recalls, "and his sidekick was a woman named Julie Halston. I had gone to college for theater and the two things I was told constantly were that I need to butch up and that I needed to lose my Bronx accent. Then here was Charles Busch getting huge laughs and applause for playing a woman, and his sidekick with this thick New York accent that sounded like me. I thought, 'Oh my god, I want to be a part of this,' and at the same time my boyfriend turned to me and said, 'You could do this!'"

"I remember feeling ashamed in that moment," she confesses. "I remember thinking that deep down I wanted to be doing that, but I didn't want anybody else to be thinking that about me. I still had so much shame about being effeminate and not butch enough."

It was an external crisis that finally provided a catalyst for Coco to shed her shame. "The activism that was happening in New York around the AIDS epidemic really motivated me to find my voice," she explains, "and I did it by creating Miss Coco Peru. I realized that there is power in owning 100 percent of who you are and really celebrating it. If they were going to call me a fag or say that I was effeminate, there was power in saying, 'Okay, you might well think I'm effeminate, but now I'm going to show you just how effeminate I can be.'"

Coco's drag name harks back to a vacation to her then-boyfriend's home country of Peru. "I was introduced to a very cute boy named Coco in a club," she remembers. "This was back in the 1980s, when you had to knock on the door and they would open a little window to check you out and see if you looked gay enough. I met this boy, Coco, and then an hour later Coco was introduced to the stage and emerged as this glamorous showgirl. He was so beautiful as a woman, and that's when I learned that he was very famous in Peru. And not just in the gay world, where you had to knock on a little door to come in, but on television. I thought it was very strange to be in a country that was so homophobic and so Catholic and yet the straight world could celebrate a man dressed as a woman … that really got me thinking about the power of just being oneself."

Coco had never performed in drag before her first solo cabaret, but she knew exactly what she wanted to do. "I called up the club and said, 'I'm going to have a show in three months and I'm booking it now,'" she recalls. "I had no doubts that I was going to find an audience. I was so bold back then. I always tell young people to make sure your goals and your vision are bigger than your fears."

"I HAD NO DOUBTS THAT I WAS GOING TO FIND AN AUDIENCE. I WAS SO BOLD BACK THEN. I ALWAYS TELL YOUNG PEOPLE TO MAKE SURE YOUR GOALS AND YOUR VISION ARE BIGGER THAN YOUR FEARS."

Coco never set out to convince the world that she was a woman. She had read about Native American two-spirit identities that resonated with her own feelings of gender fluidity and decided to incorporate that into her act. "I wanted to put that idea into Coco so I could be dressed as a woman and people would address me with female pronouns but I might be talking about my experiences as a little boy," she explains. "I wanted people to stop caring about how I identified and just relate to my story."

"I truly believe it is through storytelling that we connect with other human beings," she continues. "Storytelling changes people, and I wanted to change how people felt about me and my community. I also wanted to empower younger people. I didn't want kids to have to go through what I went through. That was my driving force. It's so corny now, but I really wanted to change the world and make it easier for the next generation. Nowadays, if I get caught up in the business side of things or get these demons about not being as commercially successful as I could be, my husband will stop me and say, 'Why did you create Coco?' And I remember that I wanted to change the world. That puts me back at the ground level of what I did and why I still do it."

Before settling on her signature style, Coco tried countless blonde and brunette wigs. "Nothing looked good on me," she laughs. "When I put the red wig on, it was so obvious in that moment that I would be a redhead. There was a lot of outrageous clown drag in New York at the time. I wanted to be the opposite. I wanted to have a simple silhouette. The flip style came simply because I did not know how to care for my wig, and every time I went to the guy that cared for it, I could see him rolling his eyes. Eventually I got so embarrassed that I had to come up with a solution that I could care for myself, and the flip was a shape that people could recognize. My drag friends like to tease me about my simple look, but I think over time they've learned to respect it when they're trying to pack these giant fucking wigs into a suitcase."

Coco's style is a nod to retro suburbia. "I love fashion from the 1950s and '60s," she says. "I remember visiting a second-hand store and finding this very plain dress. The friends I was with thought it was so ugly. They were laughing at me until I came out of the dressing room, and then they saw that it was perfect and totally Coco. I also love a bell sleeve. I grew up in the 1970s, and we had bigger sleeves then."

While she rubbed shoulders with RuPaul and Lady Bunny in the '90s, Coco was not a devotee of the downtown club kid scene. "I did Wigstock and performed in some of the clubs, but I was a cabaret performer," she explains. "I was going around from cabaret club to cabaret club handing out flyers, getting up on the open mics, telling people to come and see my show, and praying that the newspapers would come. That's how you got press back then. There was no internet, and I used to go around the city with a stencil late at night and spray, 'Miss Coco Peru. She knows!' on the sidewalks. I suppose I knew that it was illegal to do, but I guess in New York City, you just felt like you could get away with anything."

Coco remembers her nerves on the opening night of her solo show. "I was so nervous," she admits. "The weird thing is that 30 years later, I'm still terrified when I walk out on stage. One of the things drag taught me is that when you step out on stage or into the world, there's no turning back, and you just have to deliver. It's like walking off a cliff, and that is what life should be. Our fears should never stop us. You should step into the spotlight and, if you fuck up, find a way to make it work somehow."

"I used to joke that my show was like a group therapy session, only it was my turn to talk," Coco laughs. "I have had religious people come to see my show— rabbis, monks, and priests—and the funny thing is that every single one of those people said my show was like a sermon. I try to make my story universal so that as diverse as my audience may be, they feel like they can relate and we can leave with this communal energy where we feel more connected."

The idea of a breakthrough cabaret persona was partly inspired by entertainers like Bette Midler, Robin Williams, and Whoopi Goldberg, who transcended the underground and hit the mainstream. "They were people with big personalities who had to create their own career," Coco reflects. "I realized early on that I was not going to fit in a box and that I would have to create my own career, too. I've been so fortunate to be in movies and television shows, and to survive being in drag for 30 years now is kind of extraordinary."

"I always imagined that drag would become what it is today, but at the same time I cannot believe that it has," she confesses. "I remember going to Logo TV 20 years ago and pitching a show very similar to some that are on now. I was told, 'There's already one drag show on TV and we don't need anymore,' and I couldn't believe these people thought it was okay to even say that. Now drag is a lot bigger, and there is more room for other voices. I'm happy about that, because that's the world I wanted to create."

Coco does worry that there is a growing inclination to sanitize drag for the mainstream. "I always think we should be authentic and let them come to us," she says. "I remember one venue in Provincetown told me to dumb down my show. I thought, 'Don't I want to elevate people? Why do I have to be like other drag queen shows that you obviously think are dumb?' Even within our own community, that's the evolution of how we see drag."

Coco receives reams of fan mail, and if someone tells her they want to do drag, she always encourages them, even if it's just to try it. "My main advice is to be original," she instructs. "I'm starting to read a lot of comments online from young people that say things like 'Coco Peru is not a real drag queen. She doesn't even do her own makeup,' and I just find that so funny. Who are all these people who are suddenly experts on drag? Drag is whatever you chose it to be, however you chose to self-express. That is the beauty of drag."

"I always tell young people who are taking up drag as a business to show up on time," she advises. "Be respectful to the people you're working with, including technicians and bar staff. They are all there to make you look better and to make your show work."

Her final piece of advice is to not drink too much! "It's so easy to be in this scene and to believe that the drink is making you funnier," she points out, "and I'm here to tell you that it is not … Your audience deserves the best of you."

60 SECONDS WITH COCO

DESCRIBE YOURSELF IN THREE WORDS
Bitter. Bothered. Beyond.

WHERE IS YOUR SPIRITUAL HOME?
My home in Spain.

WHAT IS YOUR FAIL-SAFE PARTY TRICK?
I get everyone to tell an embarrassing shit story. Everyone has one!

WHAT WOULD YOU NEVER LEAVE THE HOUSE WITHOUT?
Lip balm.

HOW DO YOU HANDLE A CRISIS?
It runs the gamut from facing it head-on to complete denial.

WHAT IS SOMETHING NOT MANY PEOPLE KNOW ABOUT YOU?
I am an excellent parallel parker.

IF YOU RULED THE WORLD FOR A DAY, WHAT CHANGE WOULD YOU MAKE?
People who knowingly litter and pollute this planet will disappear.

SUITING UP WITH

ADAM ALL

Adam All is in many ways the godfather of the emerging generation of UK drag kings. A promoter, performer, and host known for his eccentric and debonair tailoring, Adam is one of the most recognizable faces in London, the UK, and beyond. When he's not creating weird and wacky musical parodies, he's blazing trails and nurturing brand-new performers. So button up, straighten your tie, and introduce yourself to the campiest of gents!

"I have matching accessories in almost every color, and here I've coupled my iconic pink suit with a cuddly tank top in battenberg cake hues. But which glasses to wear?"

Top: "Why be toxic and abrasive when you can be plush and gentle? This close-up shows that even subtle contour can change the perception of facial features and, therefore, gender."

Bottom: "This neon suit is easily one of my favorites. It helps me stand out, even in a traffic jam or a lineup of 7-ft drag queens."

"I'm an extremely shy person," confesses Adam, "but I've always wanted to perform. Unfortunately, I felt that looking like a shy little boy ferret probably wasn't a viable casting bracket, so I didn't think there would be an option to act except maybe as a prince or Peter Pan in a pantomime [musical comedy], but I'm still waiting to play Peter Pan."

When he was 16, Adam saw *Tipping the Velvet* on the BBC, and inspiration struck hard. "That was the first time I saw AFAB people performing masculine roles," he recalls. "Understanding that you could use your uniqueness and masculinity as a weapon and as a superpower was a huge turning point for me where I realized there was an option, even if it was a specialist thing. That was the first moment I suspected there was a career for me."

Adam began dressing in drag at the age of 17, but it would take nearly a decade before he began his legendary ascension of the cabaret ranks. "Straight after *Tipping the Velvet*, I started trying on costumes, and when I was 19, I started doing it publicly," he reveals. "I went to a huge New Year's Eve party dressed in drag. I was playing with drag throughout university and went to a couple of balls and won a few fancy dress [costume] prizes, but it was never a real performance."

"When I was 24, a drag queen in my local area said, 'I'm so bored of you going on about this. Why don't you just fucking do it, have a gig, you've got six weeks to prepare, sort your shit out!' And so my first show was a half-hour live set on a Friday night at the London Hotel, which is a notoriously difficult gig to get even now. I pooed myself but I did it, and it went down really well and I never looked back."

Adam describes himself as a cartoon-flavored ham and cheese sandwich full of nutritious masculinity. He's colorful, approachable, a little bit dumb, and always very dapper. "I think that people's drag is often a part of themselves that they've been forced to hide or adjust because society doesn't accept it," he muses. "Drag allows you to isolate those aspects and say, 'Isn't it ridiculous that I'm not allowed to be like this?'"

Out of drag, Adam used to work in very male-dominated environments, including construction, and it made him realize that the toxic masculine ideal that many men had been forced to adopt wasn't healthy or realistic for them. "On their own, most of them are nothing like that," he says. "That was the main influence that created the character of Adam All. I was also emulating people like my dad, who is a software engineer and mathematician with a gentle soul, and I wanted to celebrate that idea of maleness but present it in a very traditionally masculine look."

Adam is rarely spotted without a sensationally formal suit, but his color choices are daringly flamboyant and go way beyond what typical masculinity is meant to look like. "I like to poke fun at society's barriers," he explains, "but at the same time I'm glorifying my concept of maleness and the way I actually see it."

"I absolutely adore wearing a suit," Adam raves. "There's something almost sexual about how much I love a suit. I grew up in a very boring area in rural Hampshire, so there weren't many nice suit shops, but if Moss Bros. had a sale, then my finger streaks would be all over the window as I passed by, drooling. They would never have anything in my size because I'm so tiny, and it would drive me up the wall."

When it comes to wearing men's fashions, color is key. "It needs to be very clean and smart, but I push to choose colors that aren't usually available for men and wear them as a whole body color," Adam says. "If you go into a lot of suit shops, it's only gray, black, and blue. I find that so disturbing, that the ways a piece of material reflects and refracts light determines whether or not someone is allowed to wear it. So I like to take the suit and make it camper without that putting a question mark over Adam's masculinity."

Adam painstakingly color coordinates his outfits with those of his on-and-off stage partner Apple Derrieres, right down to his signature bow tie, glasses, and suspenders. "The glasses are empty because glass reflects light on stage, so they're all just hollow frames, but they are very much an important part of Adam's statement look," he says. "I've been able to source the majority of my suits locally in Stoke Newington, but I usually have them resized and tweaked. I've been lucky enough to find some very helpful tailors who are interested in what I do and have been extremely kind and supportive. I can get bow ties and braces [suspenders] online because they don't need to fit. For shirts, it's more of a hunting game. I like searching in places that have a huge range of stuff like vintage stores, charity shops, and discount outlet stores."

The male illusion Adam creates with his face is strikingly handsome. He always starts with a skin-matched foundation all over. "Contouring is about restructuring your face using light and shadow, so it's important to start with everything as flat and monotone as possible," he instructs. "Then I go in with a medium dark contour and shade my temples, cheekbones, and inside my eye sockets, as well as various lines on my chin and forehead. Then I go in with my darkest contour color and bring out the edges of those shaded areas to make my face more square and angular."

Facial hair isn't absolutely necessary for a drag king, but Adam sports a very suave and realistic mustache. "He's very vain," Adam says. "He likes to dress up and pamper himself. The mustache is the tipping point at which I feel very masculine and it completes the face and changes me from a boyish person into a bloke."

Adam also applies sideburns, which really help support the contouring and the squaring of the face. "I use my own hair to create my mustache and sideburns," he reveals. "I've cut my own hair since I was 16, because hairdressers don't do nonbinary cuts, or at least they didn't in the '90s, so fuck them! I just bought a pair of clippers and learned how to manage my own hair, so I just keep the trimmings and use those. I affix my sideburns with hair wax and then finish them with hairspray, but for my mustache, I use Pros-Aide adhesive because I sweat a lot and sing a lot and otherwise my mustache would end up in my mouth."

Eyebrows are also vital for Adam. Big, bushy brows can change a face from feminine to masculine in a second, so he spends a long time perfecting the large, hairy caterpillars trotting across his face. "I draw my brows on with layers of different shaded eyebrow pencil to create individual hairs," he explains. "It's quite a long process and definitely the fiddliest part of my face."

When Adam started out as a drag king, there wasn't much of a local scene, let alone a national network of like-minded artists. "There were a few kings doing stuff in their areas, and I felt strongly that having a community around you was vital for learning your trade," he insists. "I felt that it was my duty that if I had the opportunity to use a stage that I should share it with anybody else like me. I never realized quite how many people there would be until I launched BOiBOX seven years ago with my wife Apple Derrieres and people started falling out of the woodwork. It has become without doubt the biggest and proudest thing I've ever done. It's wonderful to watch the younger generation, who are just coming into the club at 18, have this broad, secure, welcoming family to step into. That's something I never had."

The range of kings out there is enormous. Adam is keenly aware that the drag queen scene is always innovating but at the same time feels there's a more recognized idea of what that innovation looks like at a given time. "Far fewer people know that the drag king scene even exists," he says, "and the limits of what a king should look

"I'VE CUT MY OWN HAIR SINCE I WAS 16, BECAUSE HAIRDRESSERS DON'T DO NONBINARY CUTS, OR AT LEAST THEY DIDN'T IN THE '90S, SO FUCK THEM!"

like or how they can perform have not yet been set. Everyone brings their own unique perspective to it. We have live singers, dancers, magicians, comedians, and fire eaters. The range of masculinity that is presented on stage isn't always necessarily a male character. Sometimes the character is nonbinary or it's an alien or it's some sort of mythical creature. People who come to the art form just know they have this masculinity or this thing society has told them is too masculine and they're sick of pretending it's wrong because of the box people want to put them in. The second they take that to the stage and celebrate it in this arena of drag, it's just everything."

"People who have never heard of a drag king before often assume that someone with a vagina can't do drag, however that person identifies," Adam says. "There's a misconception that kings are boring, that it's just a boring person impersonating a boring person and that it is ugly and not bold. There's also an assumption that the masculinity kings perform is always toxic masculinity or stereotypical masculinity. I think there's also an assumption that AFAB people can already wear whatever we like, so our drag is less subversive, and that's absolute bullshit. There are plenty of items of clothing that I'm not supposed to wear, and if I do, then people look at me oddly. There are definitely those out there who think kings just aren't as good as queens, and I'd like to poke all of those people's eyes out with sticks!"

So with its endless possibilities, can Adam begin to even define drag or the art of the king? "Drag is a palatable way of exploring gender politics with an audience who may not necessarily be ready to have some politics shoved down their throat," he reflects. "I think it's the spoonful of sugar that makes the medicine go down. It's about explaining to people that not everyone is born into a situation that is comfortable to them and that society is structured in a way that is extremely toxic for a lot of people. When you see people exploring and celebrating a part of themselves that they've had to trap away, I think that helps people to understand how some of the rules that are placed on people are damaging."

Adam believes it's important to remember that drag serves a purpose without needing to find the limelight. "I think it's really important to remember that drag is a community art form. Learning the stagecraft aspects of it is really important and learning to put on a great show rather than getting on stage and saying, 'This is me and you shall love me!' I think everybody should have the opportunity to perform in drag if they want to, but that doesn't mean that you will skyrocket to the very top after your first performance, and no one should be disappointed if that doesn't happen for them. That isn't what drag is about."

60 SECONDS WITH ADAM

DESCRIBE YOURSELF IN THREE WORDS

Gentle. Nontoxic. Flamboyant.

WHERE IS YOUR SPIRITUAL HOME?

The Royal Vauxhall Tavern. It turned out to be the kickstart of my career.

WHAT IS YOUR FAIL-SAFE PARTY TRICK?

Eating all of the sausage rolls. That's what parties are for, right? Sausage rolls?

WHAT WOULD YOU NEVER LEAVE THE HOUSE WITHOUT?

Glasses.

HOW DO YOU HANDLE A CRISIS?

I hate confrontation. I try to approach everything with kindness first.

WHAT IS SOMETHING NOT MANY PEOPLE KNOW ABOUT YOU?

I used to do synchronized swimming.

IF YOU RULED THE WORLD FOR A DAY, WHAT CHANGE WOULD YOU MAKE?

That everyone approached everything with kindness and understanding.

MYRA DUBOIS

Myra DuBois is the acid-tongued siren from South Yorkshire dreamt up by cabaret performer Gareth Joyner on a wild night out. Gareth has since grown Myra into a staple of the UK's cabaret circuit, winning her legions of loyal and adoring fans. For one night only, you're invited backstage to chat with Gareth about creating a character, dealing with hecklers, and why he's not so sure about calling Myra a drag queen.

Myra loves a leopard print, like all self-respecting Northern women.

Top: Entry-level Myra: red nails, blonde hair, and black sequins.
Bottom: Myra's creator, Gareth Joyner.

GENTLEMEN

LAD

"When I was 19, I went to a fancy dress [costume] party with my friend Richie," says Gareth, reflecting on the genesis of Myra DuBois. "We were into *Party Monster* at the time. It was the early noughties [2000s], and electro had swirled up and everybody was a club kid for five minutes. I had done a year at university in London but dropped out and went back to Rotherham to work in visual merchandising at Marks & Spencer, which was wildly less exciting.

"So, I was back within the constraints of my hometown, and Richie and I heard about a gay student night that was happening at Sheffield Hallam University. We decided we wanted to go all out and dress like, you know, knob heads! We tried to think of a theme and we settled on brides and went looking for wedding dresses in charity shops, but we couldn't find any. So the decision was landed that we would go as Rose West and Myra Hindley, respectively."

"If you look at the photograph, I don't look anything like Myra Hindley," admits Gareth. "I've got a blonde bob, a 1960s lime green dress, and some white net gloves like Mary Poppins. We had a fun night and got very battered on very cheap vodka. Following that, we sort of conversationally continued these personas. I'd ask what Rose had been up to, and Richie would say, 'She's with the kids.' Then he would ask how Myra was, and I'd say, 'Oh, she's won a tenner on the scratch cards [scratch-offs], so she's going on a caravan holiday in Ingoldmells.' It was just something we did to entertain each other."

This time also saw the rise of DIY user content on social media platforms such as Myspace and YouTube. "I was aware of videos by people like Varla Jean Merman and Jackie Beat," explains Gareth, "as well as retrospectively discovering David Hoyle's *The Divine David Presents*. These videos became part of our daily vocabulary, like conversational currency. We began to talk about Rose and Myra as these two women who had detached themselves from their infanticidal counterparts. We decided they were sisters and they lived in Rotherham. In the back of my mind, I started to buzz and think I could do videos with these girls. I could take this and make it into an act."

At the time, Gareth was working as a glass collector at a working men's club and used to watch the acts perform. "There was one singer called Lorraine Crosby," he recalls. "Her claim to fame was that she sang the female parts on Meat Loaf's 'I Would Do Anything For Love (But I Won't Do That),' and oh my god did she dine out on that. It was mentioned between every song. 'And as I said to Meat Loaf,' she would say. And I loved it! I thought it was so camp. That kind of personality started to seep into my head, and so I started to distill that into the Myra character."

That character finally began to take root when Gareth moved back to the capital. "I moved back to London in 2007 to do an arty course at Central Saint Martins, and I dropped out of that degree as well," he confesses, "but while in London, I saw an advert online for a night at Madame Jojo's called Finger In The Pie Cabaret. It was an unpaid open mic night, and I decided to do it. I went on the internet and I Googled 'how to write a joke.' I'd always been the funny one among friends, as queer kids often are as a survival tactic, but I didn't know how to structure a joke. I did a bit of research and spent ages writing a 10-minute monologue for Myra. I rehearsed it meticulously, which is funny now, because I can't remember the last time I followed a script."

"I went on stage and did this sort of version of Myra," he recounts. "If you watch it back, you can still tell it's the Myra that exists today, but it was a lot ropier. She had a leopard-print blouse and a blonde wig. The story was that she was one of these club singers that had a public incident and she had to go away from the public eye for a few years and was just getting back into the scene. It went down really well, and I got a really big laugh, which was very addictive. I went back a second time, and then they asked me to host it, and that's when the Myra snowball started to roll."

Over the years, Gareth has crafted Myra into a formidable presence with a distinct personality. "She's very egocentric and narcissistic," he explains, "but she'll have you believe she's the least narcissistic person you've ever met. Her claim is that her biggest fault is that she has too much empathy, while possessing this monstrous ego."

"There's a Terry Pratchett quote about a character, which is that she points her voice toward the end of a song and goes for it," laughs Gareth. "That really reminds me of how Myra sings. I've got a background in musical theater, but I was never quite allowed to be in the front. I think a lot of that frustration goes into Myra. I really enjoy performing songs, but I never quite found a space in which I could. If I had found some community choir at 10 years old, where people just sang for fun, I'd have had a great time and Myra probably wouldn't exist. But because I'd been told no so many times, this urge to sing was rattling around. I came up with the idea

"I'D ALWAYS BEEN THE FUNNY ONE AMONG FRIENDS, AS QUEER KIDS OFTEN ARE AS A SURVIVAL TACTIC."

that Myra is an awful singer with an unshakable belief in herself. It's become a trademark of hers."

On styling Myra, Gareth says, "For a lot of people who start drag, drag is the appeal itself. I never planned to do drag. It just so happened that I'd come up with this character who was a woman, and in order to play a woman, I had to dress up as a woman. I'm resistant to the term 'drag queen,' because nobody ever refers to my other character, Frank, as a drag *king*. Gender doesn't come into it. I feel that when people label Myra DuBois a drag queen, they're bringing my gender to the forefront of the conversation, and to me that is the least interesting thing about it. They're essentially saying, 'You have a penis though, don't you?'"

The particulars of Myra's fashion sense was inspired by actual women Gareth would see in bars and clubs, he reveals. "They would have their sparkly show outfits on, and they took one of two directions. It was either Christmas party wear from Marks & Spencer or slightly dated clothing. They would look a bit 1980s. Leopard print is the national dress of Northern women, and the blonde hair was a hangover from the Myra Hindley look, so these aspects all came together—I was never looking to other drag queens for style tips."

As for Myra's makeup look, Gareth is informed by the character herself. "Myra's face is relatively quick to throw on. It takes me about 40 minutes, because I didn't go into this trying to learn drag makeup. I went into this thinking that Myra would choose a certain color of lipstick and a certain eyeshadow and that never changes, because it's part of the character. When I auditioned for *Britain's Got Talent*, I wore a black sequined dress with a leopard-fur trim because that's what I would call entry-level Myra. If you see Myra in the black sequins and leopard print with her handbag, her red nails, and her signature sneer, it communicates something to you. My other character, Frank, always wears a shabby dated suit and a bow tie, and similarly people instantly know what world he belongs in. I tend to look at Myra as if she was a real person. That's how I tackle the aesthetic."

Gareth rarely gets cold feet before slipping them into Myra's kitten heels. "It depends how you define nerves," he offers. "There are occasional times when you're nervous and feel sick and your legs are shaking and you can't think. Or there's the sort of anticipation you feel when you're about to get on a rollercoaster that feels like a burst of adrenaline. Those sort of nerves are important to the job. I find that once I've got the costume on, I gurn [snarl] and make faces in the mirror and get myself into character. I do vocal warm-ups in character as Myra."

"There *are* occasions where it is a big deal," he admits. "I opened for Bianca Del Rio on her tour. I played the Hammersmith Apollo, which is about 3,000 seats, and I'd never played a venue that size in my life. Then for *Britain's Got Talent*, I had to do the Palladium. I was shitting myself. So I do get nerves, but I know how to harness them. Harnessing the nerves can be a productive thing, and it keeps you on your toes and in the moment."

So how does Myra deal with hecklers? "Sometimes it's someone trying to undermine the performance with a contribution of their own," Gareth considers, "but then sometimes it's just joining in. People feel they have a sense of ownership when you're an act that they go to see a lot, when you're an important fixture in their social landscape and they're familiar with your songs and routines. The benefit of Myra is that she's a very harsh persona anyway, so usually a sharp look is enough."

Gareth has a tricky relationship with Myra's politics. In the early days, she was staunchly left wing, but as he developed the persona, she became more of a cartoon, and it didn't feel right to give her any political affiliation. "I've come to realize that sincerity does not suit Myra," he admits. "If she's ever serious, it's usually in light of some awful thing that happened and people are upset. I sometimes have to let the mask slip, because I understand that Myra has a place in people's affections and a platform. Recently, a regular at the Royal Vauxhall Tavern died, and there really is only one approach to death."

"It was trickier when all the venues closed due to the coronavirus pandemic," he confesses. "One of the things the LGBTQ community felt was a sense of displacement, because a lot of the places we come together are theaters, clubs, and bars. They say that queer people get to choose their families, and a lot of the community isn't based at home with a heterosexual, two-point-four-children family unit. When the venues shut, it felt symbolic of the displacement we had been feeling for the past 10 years with the closure of so many queer venues. So that's when I felt I had to say something. It had to be in character, and it had to be heartfelt."

Gareth's top tip for any performer is to look after the dressing room. "Get there early and put a towel down," he advises. "Set your things out nicely and give yourself half an hour before you have to start putting makeup on. Give your mind room to breathe, so when it comes to getting on stage, you don't feel rushed. I'm borrowing this from *The Hitchhiker's Guide to the Galaxy*, but always have a towel in your drag bag. Whether it's to catch makeup while you're applying it or to scrub your face off at the end of the night, I find a towel is the most useful thing you can carry."

Myra's signature sneer. Usually enough to deter any hecklers.

60 SECONDS WITH MYRA

DESCRIBE YOURSELF IN THREE WORDS

Very, very famous.

WHERE IS YOUR SPIRITUAL HOME?

On stage before my followers, the AdMyras.

WHAT IS YOUR FAIL-SAFE PARTY TRICK?

I'm a total wallflower at parties. Although quite frankly, attention follows me and I can usually be found singing a note or two at people.

WHAT WOULD YOU NEVER LEAVE THE HOUSE WITHOUT?

Clothing.

HOW DO YOU HANDLE A CRISIS?

I've never noticed a crisis. Does that mean I am the crisis?

WHAT IS SOMETHING NOT MANY PEOPLE KNOW ABOUT YOU?

Nothing. I'm very famous you see, so everyone knows everything.

IF YOU RULED THE WORLD FOR A DAY, WHAT CHANGE WOULD YOU MAKE?

I'd put my shows on the NHS [National Health Service]—nourishment for the soul.

43

WEARING IT ON THE OUTSIDE WITH

GLAM-
ROU

Nonbinary drag star and theater-maker Glamrou has been changing the world for the better since 2009 with their unique blend of politics, camp theatrics, and observational comedy. Here, the sharp-witted Arabian queen talks Muslim representation, feeling the fantasy, and wearing their heart on their sleeve.

"My version of a cisgender heterosexual male actor's headshot. Taken by Lelia Scarfiotti when I performed to horny aristocrats in a palace in Venice (2017)."

Top: "Me pretending I'm startled by camera flashes when in fact I wake up to them every day."

Bottom: "Me trying to seduce your confused father. Taken by Alia Romagnoli for *Shado* magazine (2020)."

"I was raised in the Middle East until I was 11," recounts Glamrou, "between Dubai and Bahrain. I didn't have any access to queerness, and it was a really gender-segregated society. The boys hang out with their fathers and the girls hang out with their mothers. Everything is so incredibly divided, even down to where and how you pray. But I was incredibly close to my mom, and we had this really secret bond. She's very melodramatic, like a high-glamour Arabian queen, and I used to be really obsessed with her as a kid."

It wasn't until they performed in a pantomime as a young kid that Glamrou was exposed to any kind of drag. "I did a play at the British Council in Bahrain," they recall, "and I was nothing. I was asked to play a gecko of all things, but there were a couple of drag queens playing the ugly sisters, and I became obsessed with them."

"When I came to the UK and did drama at school, it became my biggest release," they reveal. "I had a lot of mental health problems throughout my life, including OCD, which was constantly overworking my brain, but weirdly, whenever I was performing, I always felt so present and so in my body and in the moment."

Glamrou attended an all-boys secondary school, where they found drama was a safe place to experiment with their self-expression. "From a young age, around 13, I was always in plays," they remember, "and whenever they needed a woman, I asked to play the woman, and it kind of just started from there."

"When I went to university and I was finally out of the parental gaze of my family—who would obviously freak out about all of this—suddenly I was like, right, I want to get into drag, and then it was as if I was on autopilot and that's when I just started a drag night. I was 19."

That was the first night of Glamrou. "It was such shit, low-budget drag," they confess, "and it was really just me being a massive bitch and telling everyone to shut the fuck up, but it was that first night in drag where you feel so yourself and happy for the first time. There wasn't much to it. I sang a song, but for the most part it was a mess. Everyone said it was a mess. My wig was falling off, my makeup was nonexistent, I was wearing something horrendous, but it was still very much an experience of liberation, and it was very powerful. I remember being with loads of my friends, who also got up in drag, and it was a really emotional night."

For Glamrou, drag is less an illusion than it is a form of authentic self-styling. "I actually don't really approach drag so much in terms of gender or that I want to dress up as a woman, feel like a woman, or make a comment on femininity," they explain. "For me, drag is taking what's inside and putting it on the outside. It's taking the stuff that you were never allowed to experience about gender and that you were told to feel shame about and putting it out there. For me, that happens to be my femininity, but it's also my being transgressive and gender nonconforming and loud and obnoxious. It's all those things. It's not about becoming a woman on stage, although I do experience a lot of gender euphoria when in drag—it's about self-expression. I think it's different for every drag artist. It's about what they have inside and what they want to put on show."

Glamrou is an eclectic persona, as serious as they are audaciously funny, and their myriad inspirations reflect that. "Even though she's a conservative Muslim woman, my mom is incredibly camp and glamorous," they divulge. "She's the kind of woman who would literally attend a picnic in a cowboy outfit thinking that's what you would need to wear to that sort of event. She is forever causing so much drama at the airport. When she couldn't get on a flight because she had brought too much luggage, she was shouting, 'This is not easy jet! This is difficult jet!'"

"So for me, on one level, my drag character is almost rescuing that image from her and queering that image for myself, and loving that for myself."

Glamrou is also inspired by Egyptian and Iraqi pop musicians. "I try to emulate stars like Umm Kulthum, who is a really famous Egyptian singer from the past. She would sing 50-minute songs and have a handkerchief in her hand and she would dab her eyes because she was so moved, and it would be really camp."

When it comes to their comedy, Glamrou is heavily influenced by characters like Valerie Cherish from the sitcom *The Comeback*. "That character is really delusional," Glamrou explains. "She thinks she's famous, but what the camera really picks up is people reading her to filth. When I approach the character of Glamrou, her comedy is all about optimism. She'll say, 'Oh my god, this guy messaged me and he said he'd love me to terrorize his hole with my thick Arab weapon!' and Glamrou thinks it's sweet that she's getting attention. I try to make Glamrou unaware of the racism she's receiving, so the audience has to think, 'Oh no, that's so tragic!'"

Exploring uncomfortable social dynamics is key to Glamrou's message when performing. After many years touring with drag supergroup Denim, enjoying successful runs at the Edinburgh Fringe and London's Soho Theatre, Glamrou decided they needed to go solo in order to get their point across.

"I wasn't really thinking about heritage or race at the beginning, because I was at an all-white university and still had a lot of anger toward my family about its attitude to homosexuality," reveals Glamrou. "I was almost actively never exploring

Islam or Arab identity, and then slowly but surely, as I joined the queer community in London, I started really hating my older work."

"In Edinburgh in our 2018 show, all the girls would get really happy claps from the audience, because it's not as threatening when a white queen is telling you to fuck off, but then suddenly I would bring up Allah and the audience would be seriously uncomfortable and I just didn't feel that safe there. That's when I decided to move on and do it alone, and I started my solo show Quran to Queen."

"I need an attentive audience for that show," they explain. "I need the safety of that because I'm exploring Arab identity and Islam. Often I'm trying to get the audience to do something a little bit racist without them realizing, and then I call them out on it, and it's a delicate tennis match. I quite like theater spaces so I can really have control in a way."

Political meaning is always at the center of what Glamrou creates for the stage. "Obviously, the act of drag always does feel inherently transgressive, but there are a lot of drag queens on TV today about whom I do think there's nothing political, and I feel they are just doing drag to feel sameness and to be number one. And I'm not saying those people shouldn't be doing drag, but for me, I'm not interested in consuming that or being affiliated with that. Just using my personal experience, drag came at a lot of personal sacrifice, especially with family."

"If I'm gonna be in front of an audience, I need to do something political and challenge something. I'm like, 'Wow, there is an audience who are willing to watch me,' so I'd better do something that's going to make people think."

"IF I'M GONNA BE IN FRONT OF AN AUDIENCE, I NEED TO DO SOMETHING POLITICAL AND CHALLENGE SOMETHING."

Glamrou rarely appears in anything short of an explosion of color. "I like to be uplifting in my aesthetic," they reveal. "That's why I love a lot of color and a lot of my looks are really celebratory. I wear a lot of Middle Eastern–influenced costume, but if I'm gonna wear a hijab or a burqa, I'll make it bright pink so it's a queer take on that. And I like it to look fake. I like the artifice. I don't worry too much about 'fishiness' or 'passability.' I want people to be aware that this is a character and a fantasy. That's why I like such sculpted wigs. I like to revel a bit in the artifice of it all."

Their advice on creating the perfect, uplifting, technicolor makeup fantasy? "The thing is, to do makeup well, you need to separate out all your brushes and have a different one for different purposes," they instruct. "Before a show, if I'm a bit more nervous or I'm in the dressing room of the Soho Theatre, sometimes I get my brushes wrong, and then all of a sudden the blending's not great. I find perfecting my hairline quite hard, because I've got such big wigs and gluing the lace down and keeping that hairline natural is quite hard. But sometimes I can't be bothered if it's a 20-minute gig at a bar and I'm running behind. I don't think people in London give a shit as much about that. I think we kind of love that messiness. That's why I hate the TV machine. It's all very 'you're not snatched enough!' and I think, 'Oh my god, you should see what I wear sometimes!'"

"I do try to clean my brushes after every use with wipes," they advise. "I was at the Edinburgh Fringe doing 20 shows in a row, and I learned the hard way that it's just not sustainable otherwise. I also find it really helpful to glue down eyebrows and draw the eyes first and then do foundation after, so that I avoid any of the makeup dribbling down into my foundation and causing a mess."

Glamrou has a big and somewhat controversial vision for the red carpet. "I would want to do Egyptian royalty," they affirm, "in a really traditional, iconic look, with Egyptian jewels like rubies, emeralds, gold, and a crown. I would enter on a throne and then have something suspicious hidden in my handbag and let people think it's a bomb, but then I release it and loads of glitter explodes everywhere!"

Above anything, Glamrou's mission is to help those around them live their best life. "What I hope is that my drag makes people think about stuff," they explain, "whether it's how colonialism brought homophobia to the Middle East or what whiteness does to people of color and how that makes people of color try to replicate whiteness. Mostly though, I want people to feel uplifted and to think, 'Okay, wow: if someone who had that hard a life with all those obstacles from family and religion is still able to get up, dress however they feel, and make people laugh, and also laugh at themselves, then no matter whatever hardship you face, you can still live your best life.'"

Their number one pearl of wisdom? "You have to fail. I probably wouldn't change anything, but I would say: don't use drag to mask who you are—use it to celebrate who you are. So much of my early drag show was me acting the part of a confident, free bitch and showing that I'm secure in my sexuality and my identity, and that's not actually how I felt on the inside at all. I was still dealing with a lot of shame and conflict and I was using drag almost as a coping mechanism, which is fine, but I think it also pays to be more truthful."

60 SECONDS
WITH GLAMROU

**DESCRIBE YOURSELF
IN THREE WORDS**

Ambitious. Neurotic.
Absurd.

**WHERE IS YOUR
SPIRITUAL HOME?**

A queer sex orgy.

**WHAT IS YOUR FAIL-SAFE
PARTY TRICK?**

To go home alone.

**WHAT WOULD YOU NEVER
LEAVE THE HOUSE
WITHOUT?**

An iconic fashion
ensemble.

**HOW DO YOU HANDLE
A CRISIS?**

By forcing every single
person I know to tell me
exactly what I want to
hear to delude myself
it's not a crisis.

**WHAT IS SOMETHING
NOT MANY PEOPLE
KNOW ABOUT YOU?**

I'm terrible at hitting on
guys. It literally terrifies
me; my legs go all jello.

**IF YOU RULED THE WORLD
FOR A DAY, WHAT CHANGE
WOULD YOU MAKE?**

I'd make the West
pay reparations for
colonialism.

GOING UNDERGROUND WITH

PEACHES CHRIST

Peaches Christ is a larger-than-life counterculture icon and the creation of B-movie connoisseur Joshua Grannell. A pioneer of the San Francisco alternative drag scene, Peaches is not afraid to raise a few eyebrows, including her own. So throw on your nastiest drag and prepare to get grungy with the godmother of camp gore as she talks queer history, shock factor, and finding your tribe!

"Peaches is more than a handful!"

"I grew up in Maryland," says Peaches. "I loved horror movies and dark things, but I felt like Hollywood was a million miles away, so it was amazing when I heard about this guy making movies in Baltimore, just up the street. *Hairspray* was a big crossover movie for John Waters, and it was in the press that the mother was played by this drag queen, Divine. I didn't know what that meant at the time, but slowly I started to figure it out. I remember that I had to downplay my interest, because I knew it was a tell of my queerness, so I was secretly obsessed with *Hairspray* and it blew me away. Divine blew me away, and shortly after that I discovered Frank-N-Furter and *The Rocky Horror Picture Show*, so my entrance to the world of drag was through cult movies."

This passion for movies drove Peaches to college and ultimately a renewed sense of identity. "I left Maryland and went to study film production at Pennsylvania State," she recounts, "and there I came out of the closet and started to become involved in queer activism. Club kid culture was a very big thing in the early '90s, so I started dabbling in club kid looks and we would drive to New York or Pittsburgh and go out to these nightclubs."

Peaches herself was a happy accident, born on the spur of the moment in 1995. "I was making my senior thesis film *Jizzmopper*," she recalls, "and as we were shooting, the guy playing the drag queen character didn't show up to set. We were shooting on 16mm film, which was very expensive for us. It was more money than I had ever spent on anything, and this guy was not only fucking up our time but losing us money, so I stepped in and played the part. Her name was originally Coco, but we changed it to Peaches. So my first time doing drag was in my own movie."

When it came time to promote the movie, Peaches dragged up to hand out flyers on campus. "At that time, it was really shocking to see someone in drag in central Pennsylvania," she remembers. "It was dangerous. I got pushed around and harassed, but I loved it. I loved the transgressive shock value that drag had."

"When I graduated, I had no money, no job, and nowhere to live," she admits, "and yet I still got on a plane to San Francisco. When I arrived, there was a nightclub that had just started that was really the center of the alternative drag scene. It was called Trannyshack, and I became a performer at that cabaret. It was Tuesdays at midnight, and it lasted for years and years and became very successful. It was very inclusive of drag queens, but also trans women, nonbinary folk, and even heterosexual transvestites who would come with their wives, and everybody fit into this world of outsiders. Peaches Christ was really born there."

"A queen with a crown of thorns."

After a few years at Trannyshack, Peaches launched her own sister show. "My friend Hecklina was the mistress of Trannyshack," she explains, "and I hosted Midnight Mass, which was a late-night movie event in a cinema, and they both became very popular together. We really created that whole scene at the time."

The persona of Peaches Christ is the Glamazonian, feminine cartoon creature that little Joshua had to suppress for many years. "She's very much the fantasy of femininity that I admired in women like Tura Satana, Elvira, and Joan Crawford," she observes, "mixed with the horror of Freddy Kruger and Norman Bates. I don't think of Peaches as a woman, and I don't think of her as a man. I think of her as some sort of expression of outrageousness that defies gender in a way."

Many people are surprised to learn that out of drag, Peaches is pretty introverted. "I love collaborating with a close circle, but I don't always like to be the center of attention," she confesses. "I enjoy standing on the sidelines and observing. However, as Peaches, once I have that battle armor on, I'm able to be that other persona. It sort of unlocks this channel of creativity and self-confidence."

Peaches' personal style is a delicious mixture of hilarious and horrifying. "It's no secret that Peaches' face was obviously inspired by Divine," she admits, "although it's nowhere near as cool or as polished as what Divine and Van Smith came up with together when they were creating the character. One thing I remember reading was that John Waters and Divine really loved this idea of Elizabeth Taylor meets Pogo the Clown. I think what I did was to take that more in the direction of Pogo than Liz Taylor. I've had people paint me with more natural features, and what's funny is I just don't look like Peaches, and people don't like it."

Before the glossy tutorials of YouTube and Instagram, underground performers were forced to improvise makeup techniques with materials they found in theatrical stores. "We used to use putty," Peaches recalls. "I used to put putty over my eyebrows and that was so annoying, so when someone younger suggested Elmer's glue, we were all so grateful. Now I'll do the glue and set that with powder, but I'm so paranoid

"I DON'T THINK OF PEACHES AS A WOMAN, AND I DON'T THINK OF HER AS A MAN. I THINK OF HER AS SOME SORT OF EXPRESSION OF OUTRAGEOUSNESS THAT DEFIES GENDER IN A WAY."

"Blood, bath, and beyond."

about my brows popping out that I'll also do a thin layer of spirit gum. Once you get that on there, those eyebrows are not going anywhere. Of course, at the end of the night, it takes a little extra time to remove."

For silhouettes, Peaches likes to refer to vintage fashion images. "Christian Dior is a big influence on a lot of the stuff that I do," she explains, "as well as old Hammer Horror and Hollywood films of the 1950s. What we do is to overexaggerate everything to make it larger than life. Joan Crawford is also a huge influence on my shoulder pads and jackets and on the mix of masculine and feminine."

Peaches is also a fan of mashups, collaborations, and intertextuality. One of her most famous appearances is as a Peaches Cenobite in the style of the classic horror movie *Hellraiser*. "I worked with a makeup artist and a costume designer," she says, "and together the three of us came up with this gown where the costume designer did all the leather and contraptions but the makeup artist created flayed breasts and nails coming out of my head, so that was a very satisfying experience."

"I first wore the Cenobite outfit to the San Francisco Symphony Hall. I was hosting an evening of horror music for Halloween. The fact that Peaches has collaborated with the San Francisco Symphony for years now is surreal. It is one of the finest orchestras and most snotty institutions in the world, so for me to show up on stage with flayed tits was a big deal. It made a lot of people very uncomfortable, but then again I think that's what drag does best."

"I was lucky that I grew into drag culture through cult movies," she muses, "so I got to seek out those interests and that's how I was introduced to The Cockettes, Richard O'Brien, Tim Curry, Vivienne Westwood, and the punk scene of London. I also grew up admiring Jackie Beat, Coco Peru, Lady Bunny, and RuPaul. RuPaul was very punk rock at a certain time."

One thing Peaches credits for her success is that she had to figure out everything on her own. "We had to come up with our own inspirations," she explains, "so if you look at my generation of performers, I think you see that our styles and performance strengths are very unique to who we are. That's changed a bit now; you have this school of drag culture. There are young people now who grow up watching one TV show and learning what drag should be. I know I'll probably get in trouble for saying this, but I honestly feel like the more popular it becomes, the more cookie cutter it becomes, and that's inherently less interesting. There's a mass ability to consume things so that everybody learns to contour the same way, whereas in my day, we were terrible at makeup and I'm actually really grateful for that."

Peaches admits she never would have imagined drag becoming as popular as it has. "I remember going to the first DragCon with Coco Peru," she recalls. "She and I were walking around saying, 'Can you believe this?'"

So what does that mean for the individual impact artists can make in a modern landscape? "Even a few years ago, I would have told you that drag is always political," Peaches ventures. "I think because we've reached a zenith of popularity that I could not have foreseen in my lifetime, I'm starting to reevaluate that. I'm not slamming any artist, but the reality of it is that what was once the truly transgressive, alternative, underground culture has now become the pumpkin-spice latte of pop culture. I named myself Peaches Christ after Jesus, because I wanted to piss people off. People ask me if I know that that is offensive. Well yeah, of course I know. I had to go to Catholic school. I was told I was going to hell. I was told my being gay was a perversion, so for me, taking the name Christ was a political act."

"I will say this. Until the gender binary is erased, until misogyny is erased, until homophobia is erased, drag will continue to be political. All we have to do is look at the rise of fascism and the global shift toward the right to see this whole dark cloud of conservatism that is disgusted by what we do. Until that is fixed, I believe drag will continue to have a political component."

"UNTIL THE GENDER BINARY IS ERASED, UNTIL MISOGYNY IS ERASED, UNTIL HOMOPHOBIA IS ERASED, DRAG WILL CONTINUE TO BE POLITICAL."

Unjaded by the zeitgeist of drag today, Peaches is a champion of emerging queer talent. "I think young artists today have a different challenge, which is figuring out how to be unique in a saturated landscape," she reflects. "It's easy for me, as someone who was in a much smaller pool, to, say, be unique. When I started out in the '90s, there were no spooky drag queens. All I can say is follow your gut. What are you passionate about? What are you good at? If you suck at making wigs, fuck it! Who cares? I think this idea that a drag performer has to be good at everything is overrated. I think you should be good at a few things and good at asking for help with the rest."

On where drag is headed next, Peaches remarks, "I'm expecting a drag queen to run for political office in the near future. That seems like the next step. We just elected Honey Mahogany in San Francisco to a seat on the Democratic County

Central Committee. I think that's the future of drag: taking it out of the nightclubs and putting it center stage."

So can we expect a Peaches for President ticket in the near future? "Maybe. I don't know. I have to say that I come from a very political family. My brother is a diplomat. My mother worked on Capitol Hill. My sisters worked for senators, so it's always been part of the family. I would have said no in the past, but I think because of the state of the world right now, it's like, I know that I would make a better fucking president than the one we have. I would not have considered it 10 years ago, but nowadays I'm like, 'Yeah, maybe I should.'"

Asked for a campaign slogan, she simply offers: "I'd make a better president than that asshole!"

"I KNOW THAT I WOULD MAKE A BETTER PRESIDENT THAN THE ONE WE HAVE."

Top left: "Impresario and horror hostess Peaches Christ may give

60 SECONDS WITH PEACHES

DESCRIBE YOURSELF IN THREE WORDS
Creative. Funny. Audacious.

WHERE IS YOUR SPIRITUAL HOME?
The beach.

WHAT IS YOUR FAIL-SAFE PARTY TRICK?
I can say the Hail Mary in French. Thank you, Catholic school!

WHAT WOULD YOU NEVER LEAVE THE HOUSE WITHOUT?
My phone. Ugh, I love and hate it but can't live without it!

HOW DO YOU HANDLE A CRISIS?
I'm fairly good in a crisis, able to get perspective and jump into action.

WHAT IS SOMETHING NOT MANY PEOPLE KNOW ABOUT YOU?
I'm introverted.

IF YOU RULED THE WORLD FOR A DAY, WHAT CHANGE WOULD YOU MAKE?
I would replace all of the world's cis male leaders with women.

Dance, Dynamism, and

FIERCE

Death-Defying Stunts

These high-kickers and dancing daredevils embody a powerful, high-energy stagecraft. Fierceness is all about killer lip-syncs and crowd-pleasing gymnastic abilities. Expect flipping, dipping, and hair-whipping that would make a pop diva blush. Be warned: these showgirls are not for the faint of heart!

SNATCHING WIGS WITH
FREIDA SLAVES

Freida Slaves is the unapologetically bearded belle of the UK drag circuit. She has featured in music videos for Sporty Spice and Little Mix and appeared in all her towering glory on dozens of red carpets and at countless awards shows. A fearsome and dynamic dancer, Freida creates routines that never fail to bring the house down and leave the audience thirsty for more. Gird your loins for one girl who knows a thing or two about liner, lip-syncs, and letting her hair down.

"Taken at DragWorld, where I was sponsored by an alcohol company to attend and drink all day. Easiest job ever. Outfit by Bang London, who have made costumes for Beyoncé!"

"Taken while hosting at Bafta's pre- and aftershow parties for Virgin Media. Hence all the red. Wig sculpted by Weekday Wigs."

"I first discovered drag through the television," recalls Freida. "I grew up with Lily Savage and Dame Edna, but I didn't fully understand that they were drag queens. I just knew them as funny people with funny hair and costumes, a bit like Mr. Blobby. When I got older, I learned what drag queens were and I was bloody scared of them! I wouldn't walk down Old Compton Street, because I had a genuine fear of drag queens. Thinking back on it, I expect it was because I was definitely in the closet. I knew that I was gay and I didn't want them to call me out on my gayness. That's where my fear stemmed from, but also I don't like to get called out in any situation. I don't like going to stand-up, as I always get picked on because I'm the tallest in the crowd, and I don't like attention in that way."

Like many millennial megababes, Freida gained a deeper understanding of the art of drag from watching *RuPaul's Drag Race*. "That's when I realized it wasn't just scary old men in sequined dresses calling you gay between Shirley Bassey numbers," she admits. "I realized that there were different forms of drag. Even though *Drag Race* isn't that diverse, it's still more diverse than what I had an idea of growing up."

Freida grew up in East Oxford, which she describes as "super liberal, really chill, and very nice," before adding that it's "a nice place to grow up, but not a great place to be once you are a teenager." Starved of cultural stimulation and creative outlets, she left for dance school when she was 15, first to Cambridge and then on to London.

Freida's first genuine encounter with drag queens happened while she was mixing them drinks in her part-time job at London's National Theatre. Iconic queer venue The Glory had taken over the outdoor River Stage, overlooking the Thames River, for a whole weekend.

"They were all in the bar causing an absolute bloody riot," she remembers. "That was the first time I had actually interacted with drag queens, and I realized right away that was what I wanted to do, because they were all so lovely. They were just having the time of their lives pissing about on stage, and I thought, 'I want to do that!'"

Freida soon followed her newfound friends onto the amateur competition circuit, entering The Glory's annual drag queen tournament, Lip-Sync 1000. "I was absolutely riddled with nerves," she confesses. "I was swearing, I was shaking, and I couldn't put my bloody nails on. I had to call my friend to come down to the dressing room to help me. I don't know why I was quite so nervous, because I'm a performer anyway, but I think because it was something new, it felt like a big risk. All of my friends were there, and I was competing alongside big names that I looked up to in the drag world. As soon as they called my name and I stepped out onto the stage, I got a bigger rush than I've ever had performing anything else. I knew then that I had found my home and that this was something I was going to be doing for a long time."

Freida trained classically in jazz, tap, and ballet, with the latter as her strongest form, but she joined the professional world as a commercial dancer, where the jobs were easier and more fun. "I try to incorporate all of my training into drag," she explains, "not just in terms of performance, but also professionalism. In the dance world, you have to turn up on time, be polite to everyone, and stay quiet during rehearsal. I feel like some drag performers are missing that. You can definitely tell a trained performer from their mannerisms and how they treat everyone."

When it comes to learning a lip-sync, Freida's top tip is to listen to the audio track on repeat. "It's not just about learning the words," she stresses, "it's also about learning where to breathe. I saw an amazing drag queen do a three-minute lip-sync of Barbara Streisand drinking, talking, and smoking. That's all they do for three minutes, and it's absolutely incredible to watch. You also need to pay attention to the emotions in the track. Once you know your intentions, it's easier to place the words and it looks like you're actually living through the audio rather than just going through the motions. That's the difference between a great lip-syncer and someone who just knows all the words. Also, when I lip-sync, I tend to sing along, but very quietly. If you turned the music off, you'd hear a lot of very loud whispering and lip smacking, which is not sexy at all!"

When it comes to fashion, Freida doesn't recommend splashing the cash. "I started out with really cheap shit and I still wear cheap shit," she laughs. "It's usually a leotard with all sorts of things attached to it. My style revolves around dance, so I always need my legs to be free. I need to be able to do high kicks and spins and turns without getting tangled up in tassels. My look is really inspired by the 1990s. I wear lots of black straps and gold paired with hip-hop clothing like bandanas, crop tops, and baggy trousers."

"The first wig and outfit I ever made for myself for a Diana Ross–themed party. This became a staple Freida pose, because if I didn't hold all the hair back I'd be consumed by it and resemble Cousin Itt."

"IT'S NOT JUST ABOUT LEARNING THE WORDS, IT'S ALSO ABOUT LEARNING WHERE TO BREATHE ... WHEN I LIP-SYNC, I TEND TO SING ALONG, BUT VERY QUIETLY."

The one thing Freida does incorporate into all of her looks is her iconic chains. "I'm known for black, gold, and chains, which is great because it's like a uniform," she says. "People have actually pointed to other queens wearing black with gold chains and said they look like Freida Slaves, which I actually love, because I've always liked the idea of signatures in my look. Mr. T said he wore gold chains as a symbol of his African heritage. He said, 'I've turned steel chains into gold to symbolize the fact that I'm still a slave, only my price tag is higher.' That's why I've always worn chains. I think people just think they look pretty, but that's what they mean to me."

While she's not one to mix current affairs with pleasure, Freida believes that the sheer unapologetic matter of her visibility always carries a message. "Drag for me is a form of escapism," she reveals. "I just want to dance to a club hit for three minutes, live my best life, and then invite you all to live your best lives with me. However, drag is always political. You can't get away from it, and that's what I love about drag. I don't need to get on stage and lip-sync Boris Johnson or Donald Trump, because that's not my style of drag. However, for me to stand there as a black man in women's clothes in a predominantly white club is political. That's just what it is without me trying."

Freida is famous for hair so enormous it would make Diana Ross blush, often appearing in voluminous afro pieces or braided weave down to her thighs. Her fascination with hair goes all the way back to her childhood. "When I was five years old, I had a girlfriend," she recalls. "She had the most humongous blonde hair ever, and I was just obsessed with it. I was also obsessed with the Little Mermaid and how her red hair moved in the water. I wanted to be a hairdresser. That passion has come with me into my old age. I think it could be the knowledge that I can't grow my own hair long. I'm starting to go bald now, so everything I want and everything I can't have, the long hair, the big curly afro hair, goes into Freida."

"I make all my hair myself," Freida reveals. "I taught myself by watching tutorials online. It's mostly simple braiding and crocheting like you would do with

"DRAG FOR ME IS A FORM OF ESCAPISM. I JUST WANT TO DANCE TO A CLUB HIT FOR THREE MINUTES, LIVE MY BEST LIFE AND THEN INVITE YOU ALL TO LIVE YOUR BEST LIVES WITH ME."

natural hair. I have found the process really therapeutic, and that's how I started out really. Before I was a drag queen, I would braid hair to pass the time, so that has really helped me out."

Between the color palette, chains, heavy nods to Versace and Thierry Mugler, and massive hair, Freida has created a highly recognizable brand and it isn't a wheel she plans to reinvent any time soon. "I'm too lazy to change my style much," she jokes. "As I see it, I'm a product, and that's what people want and expect. When I first started, I had a massive issue of worrying what people might think of me in each performance. The first time I was booked to do a really big show, I really went through it worrying about what I was going to do. Then someone said to me, 'You're booked to do you, so just do you!' And that was the best possible advice. Being myself has worked all this time, so I'm not going to change it drastically unless I get really bored of it."

Freida came to drag with a well-stocked toolkit from her theatrical background, including some degree of makeup training. "I knew how to plaster it on and paint for the back row," she recalls. "I also used to watch a lot of makeup tutorial videos to fall asleep because I find them so soothing, then I would try a lot of those looks on my own face and work out what worked for me and what didn't. People forget that we all have different-shaped faces, especially differently shaped eyes and lips. You need to see what works for you, pick and choose from different techniques, and then create your own signature paint from that."

The classic Freida face comprises razor-sharp eyeliner that covers her entire brow bone and shoots all the way up to her temples. "Always draw outward and upward for a feline-looking face," she recommends. "Everything should point from the center of the nose up to the temples, so it looks like you've had a mini face lift. My face is essentially big eyeliner snatched upward and my beard."

And what does the beard mean for Freida? "I'd like to say I'm making a political point by keeping my beard," she muses, "but the true fact is that I look like a thumb without it and I only live as Freida for about 10 percent of my time, so I want to give the boy some help, too. It's literally just shallow, aesthetic reasons. Sorry to disappoint. Drag is a performance, but I'm also a human being and I'm not going to change my whole appearance for five minutes on stage, even if they're the best five minutes of my life."

When it comes to advice for newer queens, there are two tidbits Freida likes to serve. "Firstly, always do your squats, because then you don't have to pay for padding," she instructs. "I don't pad, but people always comment on my butt, so the extra reps are definitely worth it."

"My final tip is to always spray perfume on your hair and your hands so people think that you smell nice, even if you're a sweaty bitch like me. I sweat so much on stage and then I stink, but if you spray perfume on your hands, when you point into the crowd or touch the audience, they'll think you smell delicious."

"ALWAYS SPRAY PERFUME ON YOUR HAIR AND YOUR HANDS SO PEOPLE THINK THAT YOU SMELL NICE, EVEN IF YOU'RE A SWEATY BITCH LIKE ME."

"Outtakes from a parody of a Sugababes video that I shot with Crystal and BabyLame, my drag dad."

60 SECONDS WITH FRIEDA

DESCRIBE YOURSELF IN THREE WORDS

Thicc. Furry. Cheap.

WHERE IS YOUR SPIRITUAL HOME?

At the bottom of a Jaffa Cakes box.

WHAT IS YOUR FAIL-SAFE PARTY TRICK?

Twerking in a headstand. Think yoga, but make it ho. Hoga? I'm trademarking that.

WHAT WOULD YOU NEVER LEAVE THE HOUSE WITHOUT?

A spare pair of underwear.

HOW DO YOU HANDLE A CRISIS?

A box of Jaffa Cakes.

WHAT IS SOMETHING NOT MANY PEOPLE KNOW ABOUT YOU?

I once was on a ship that was under the threat of pirates, so we had to take turns on lookout with a high-pressure water gun.

IF YOU RULED THE WORLD FOR A DAY, WHAT CHANGE WOULD YOU MAKE?

I'd make sure unbiased, factual BAME history is taught in schools; all world leaders [are] womxn; and the first two Spice Girls albums [are] mandatory listening.

TRIPPING OUT WITH

FAY LUDES

Psychedelic bimbo clown Fay Ludes is a campy, larger-than-life show host and high-energy dance sensation. When she's not blazing trails and nurturing the next generation of talent, she can be found traveling the world with a suitcase full of orange wigs and enviable vintage fashions. So cast your mind back to Studio 54 and let Fay take you on the trip of a lifetime as she talks hijinks, high kicks, and even higher hair.

"I love a loud and proud Pride look! This was shot in Denver while I was there performing during their Pride. I ordered a wig that didn't come on time, but Denver queen Jessica L'Whor came through."

"Baby's first professional photos! These were the first professional images taken of me in drag. I wanted to showcase my vintage glam, but also a bit of edge as well."

"I had a pen pal in high school whose sister would let her use her ID, and she would go out to clubs in San Francisco and snap photographs with drag queens and club kids and mail them to me," Fay remembers. "So as a teenager, I had photos of drag queens on my bedroom wall. That friend was the first person I came out to and I thought she was the coolest, but she had a crush on my best friend, so it was a whole lesbian love triangle. In 1995, there weren't as many weirdos, so we all kinda had to stick together."

Somewhat surprisingly for someone who has been around drag for decades, Fay only donned the lace front about three years ago. "I moved to Chicago four years ago," she explains, "and I was looking for people to go to drag shows with, and a queen here asked me why I didn't just do drag. I didn't think anything would come of it, being AFAB and older. I thought that I would like to do it but didn't know if there would be space for me in the community."

Fay identifies as nonbinary and uses "they/them" pronouns in day-to-day life, so drag was a way for her to channel a hyper-feminine persona on her own terms. "I feel like Fay is kind of the character that I had been putting on throughout my early 30s just trying to survive being read as female," she reveals. "She started out wearing my clothes, because my wardrobe was all vintage. So Fay was basically an offshoot of a person who already existed. I now see her as a character I was using because I felt suffocated by the expectations of femininity as a female-bodied person."

Fay's persona is high kitsch, but her name is a reference not everybody gets right away. "Quaaludes were a very popular party drug that people were taking at Studio 54," Fay explains, "and I wanted to do a pun on that. I travel a lot for shows and people don't necessarily get the name, because Quaaludes have been off the market since the 1980s. I think they were called lemons in the UK."

After a few months of rubbing up against all the right shoulders on Chicago's drag circuit and turning up in fabulous looks to support other artists, Fay took the plunge. "For my first performance, I did a whole number around Quaaludes," she remembers. "I made a skirt embellished with pills and rhinestoned everything. I did 'Just Like A Pill' by Pink mashed up with a bunch of quotes from *The Wolf of Wall Street*. I took a ton of pills and spit them all over the audience. Looking back, it wasn't a bad debut. It could have been a lot worse."

Overall, the Chicago scene has been very welcoming. "There is still a little bit of tokenism," she acknowledges, "wherein each show wants queers of color, one king, and one AFAB performer, and sometimes that is all the same person. That being said, I felt very lucky that within a year of doing drag I sorted out which direction I wanted to go in. I work at Hamburger Mary's, which is a chain of drag restaurants, and I'm the first AFAB performer to have a show host position across around 15 locations. When I first started showing up at Hamburger Mary's, they were very confused by me. They were like, 'Oh, so you're a woman that does drag?'"

For the most part, people have been really receptive. "The times where I'm more nervous about it are when I travel," she admits. "There is always that fear that they don't know that I'm AFAB, because it's not something that I advertise. I don't do transformation videos. There are people who have followed me for years, and then they've met me and been surprised that I'm not a man, and I'm like, 'Yeah, but you enjoyed my stuff online, so it doesn't really matter!' I did have one club in Chicago book me and I was surprised, because they didn't have a history of being supportive to AFAB queens, so I got very nervous. I asked a friend of mine, who assured me the venue knew, but when I got there, everybody backstage was clearly uncomfortable and they never booked me again. So that's frustrating."

Fay believes that people have spent too much time focusing on gender when it comes to a queer art form that is essentially about gender. "It's queer art that you can use to express yourself," she explains. "My daytime look and Fay Ludes' have nothing in common. I am actually a little more on the masculine scale during the day and I use Fay to channel the small amount of femininity that I have. I think that people should be able to display and send up gender however they see fit, no matter what is underneath. It should be about transforming yourself into something otherworldly."

Fay likes to refer to herself as a psychedelic bimbo clown and dress accordingly. "I love glamour, ruffles, rhinestones, and anything with a bit of a vintage feel," she reveals. "I grew up lower income, so I've never had a ton of money to spend on drag. You have to figure out what's worth spending on and what isn't. I perform between four and six days a week and I'm expected to consistently have new outfits,

"PEOPLE SHOULD BE ABLE TO DISPLAY AND SEND UP GENDER HOWEVER THEY SEE FIT, NO MATTER WHAT IS UNDERNEATH. IT SHOULD BE ABOUT TRANSFORMING YOURSELF INTO SOMETHING OTHERWORLDLY."

so I can't buy a $200 custom drag outfit every day. Typically, my rule is that if I can't make the money back in one show, then I don't want it."

"I shop a lot online," she says. "I go and look at vintage dance costumes from the 1970s and '80s, things that aren't clockable as dance costumes but look cute with some rhinestones added. One of my outfits that people go bonkers for was a $13 jumpsuit I bought online and put about 3,000 rhinestones on. People gag every time I wear it! I love strolling into the club in an outfit that was under $50 and having people compliment me on it, and I am fully that girl who will say, 'Oh, it was $10!'"

Fay's thriftiness extends to her approach to wigs. "I think a lot of the wigs you can buy for $30–$40 from generic online retailers are absolutely fine," she says. "I've also realized that I hate styling wigs. This is a mistake a lot of people make. You need to figure out what you can do on your own and what it is worth having someone else do. I don't think you should have someone else do everything for you, because part of the art is participating in the creation of the look, but you don't need to do everything. Wigs are one of the things I tend to outsource."

So where does Fay store her extensive collection of costumery? "I moved into my own place because I have so much drag," she laughs. "I live in a one-bedroom apartment and I'm using the bedroom as a drag room, and my bed is in the dining room. I have hanging racks in my drag room so I can hang stuff from the ceiling, and there's a whole wall of industrial shelving, shelves for my travel cases and styled wigs, and a desk with a makeup station. I think I've used the space pretty well."

Fay's top tip for traveling with wigs is to source boxes with structure to protect the hair on all sides. "If it's a plastic box, poke a hole in it, because if it gets steamy in there, it can take the style out of the wig," she explains. "When you take your wig off after a gig, let that bitch breathe for a little bit and don't pack her up straight away, because that sweat and the heat from your head is going to ruin the style if you put it straight in a sealed plastic container."

Fay's makeup is bright, campy, and clownish, with a signature exaggerated lip. "I line my bottom lip first, then mark out a cupid's bow just above my own," she explains. "I draw little points at the corners of my mouth. Then I extend the bottom line to meet those points and go back up over the top lip. The hardest part is getting the top lip into the cupid's bow at just the right angle. My lips are usually slightly uneven, but I figure if I keep my mouth moving, nobody notices too much!"

Drag gives Fay the outlet to express herself and command the attention that she enjoys, which balances out her quieter side. "I get to dress up and look extravagant and have people tell me I look sickening and throw money at me," she laughs. "On the flip side, I can be an introverted hermit, so drag is actually quietening a lot of my demons, because my need to be bold and extravagant is channeled into one thing, and then I can come home and be a human being. I come from a theater and dance background with a huge love of the performing arts, and drag married that with human interaction. There's something about the night life and clubs where you get to be part of a community as well. When you bridge the community with the performance aspect, I think it's just perfect. Drag plays a big role in bringing queer communities together and gives people a reason to congregate and celebrate queer art."

A quintessential Fay Ludes number is four minutes of sucker-punch energy. "I love a reveal. I typically come in very poised and dramatic, and then rip that off and do high kicks and splits, which is getting harder to do at my age, but I am best known as a high-energy performer," she says. "One of my favorite moments was performing over in the UK. I did a number I made in response to someone telling me I couldn't do drag because I was AFAB. I was performing in a basement and I was freaking out because the ceiling was so low. In the last part of the song, the audience joined in with the Beyoncé choreography from 'Run the World (Girls).' I was so overwhelmed that I cried when I got off stage because the reception was so beautiful and I felt so accepted in that moment. That's coming from someone who has a lot of demons around queerness, because I grew up an evangelical Christian and my parents are republican Trump supporters, so there's a lot of guilt I've had around my queerness, and to feel truly loved in that moment brought me so much joy."

Fay runs an amateur competition night every Tuesday in Chicago, and many of the performers are under 21, as it's one of the limited spaces they can perform. A lot of people do their debut at her show, so she is used to dealing with nervous new drag performers.

"I like to remind people that drag is meant to be fun," she stresses. "Every single person in that audience is there to have a good time. Nobody is there to see if you fuck up or do a bad job. Nobody wants you to fail. Everybody is there to support queer art, and even if you fuck up, they're going to be understanding. Drag doesn't have to be life or death, and one show won't ruin your whole career. Try to loosen the fuck up, because honestly, it's drag. It's not that serious."

"I turn a new look every week at my Tuesday show at Hamburger Mary's. Queens love a backstage shot, so here's one of mine!"

60 SECONDS WITH FAY

DESCRIBE YOURSELF IN THREE WORDS

Psychedelic bimbo clown.

WHERE IS YOUR SPIRITUAL HOME?

Anywhere my dog is.

WHAT IS YOUR FAIL-SAFE PARTY TRICK?

I do a leg extension and jump into the splits, and the crowd goes wild!

WHAT WOULD YOU NEVER LEAVE THE HOUSE WITHOUT?

Giant vintage sunglasses.

HOW DO YOU HANDLE A CRISIS?

I'm quite calm in a crisis if I'm helping someone else. If it's something I did wrong, I'm a mess!

WHAT IS SOMETHING NOT MANY PEOPLE KNOW ABOUT YOU?

I skipped a grade in school.

IF YOU RULED THE WORLD FOR A DAY, WHAT CHANGE WOULD YOU MAKE?

Free healthcare for all. Reparations for the black community. Housing would be a right, not a privilege. The police system would be abolished.

CALYPSO JETÉ BALMAIN

Spinning, vogueing, high-kicking queen Calypso is a force to be reckoned with and never anything short of a full production. She has one stiletto heel firmly planted in the glitzy world of high drag and another making waves in the underground ballroom scene. Here, she tells us about navigating gender presentation, making costumes from scratch, and how to land the perfect death drop—just don't ever call it a death drop!

"Whether there's just one person in the audience or a million, give every performance your all."

C alypso Jeté Balmain is a formidable name in the ranks of the ballroom circuit, a world first revealed to mainstream audiences in the 1990 documentary film *Paris Is Burning* and more recently illustrated in the drama series *Pose*. "Ballroom is basically a series of underground functions where you compete in various categories," Calypso explains. "Ballrooms were originally underground safe havens for black, Latino, gender nonconforming, and transgender individuals. Balls stemmed from the trans and drag pageant circuit."

"In ballroom, my main category is face," she says. "It's a category where I walk straight up to the judging table to show off my facial features, and then they get a little closer and even touch my face. Do I have nice features? Do I have nice teeth? Do I have a lot of makeup on? Can you see the structure of my face from the back of the runway?"

"The other categories I walk in are drag performance, runway, sex siren, realness, and vogueing," she reveals. "You know Madonna's 'Vogue'? That's referencing an early style of vogueing based on creating symmetry and mimicking poses like those seen in *Vogue* magazine. It has evolved since then into more exaggerated movements that vary from soft, graceful, and fluid (like melting on the floor) to controlled, rapid, and dramatic (think high-energy stunts)."

"For the first ball I ever walked, I entered every category, because I wanted to really put myself out there," she confides. "When you start out in ballroom, you start out in virgin categories. At my first ball, I won virgin vogue and virgin face. After that, I started walking more face. I've never lost a face and I beat two legends in the face category, so that's my main category now."

"As well as categories, we have different statuses within ballroom," she explains. "There's star, statement, and legend. Stars are upcoming names in ballroom. Statement is when you've been around for a while, so that's like, 'Okay, we see you.' Then you have legends like King Amiyah Scott, who is legendary for face. Beyond that, you also have icons, so an example of an icon within ballroom would be Leiomy Maldonado. I'm currently working my way toward legendary icon status."

Before ascending the ranks of the ballroom underground, Calypso had already started making a name for herself as a fierce performer on the club and show circuit, stunning audiences with her pop-culture-heavy dance and lip-sync routines. She is famed for giving her all to performances and creating long-lasting impressions.

"Janelle Monae is somebody I really look up to," says Calypso. "She's always engaging with the audience, so when I'm doing drag shows, I like to interact with the crowd. I'm not the type of girl to just sit there and perform and collect my tips. I like to put on a show. No matter if there's one person or a million people watching, you're going to get the same amount of energy."

"I've taken everything I've learned in drag shows and brought that back to ballroom," she explains. "When I come out for a ball, I'm always giving you extra so that people say, 'Wow, she's coming in from the ceiling!' Or I'm being carried in. I always want the audience to be inspired and to have something to remember."

It's this attitude and dedication that makes Calypso such a force to be reckoned with. "Ballroom is more about creating those memories than it is about the actual win," she reveals. "If you make a memory, it lasts a lot longer, because people can look back at an iconic performance and want to recreate that. I can't tell you how many balls I've won, but it's outnumbered by the moments I've had."

Calypso is one of countless women who perform as drag queens, defying the misconception that male-identified people have any kind of ownership of what it means to be a queen. As a nightclub performer, she may find herself mostly among gay men, but in ballroom, trans identities are far more present and celebrated.

"I started transitioning last year," she explains. "When I first started out in drag, I used to paint very heavy, with big eyes and exaggerated contour. But a drag queen in ballroom is very different from a drag queen you might see on TV. They don't paint huge features and wear 10 pairs of lashes stacked on top of each other. It's more about *softening* the features."

It is the sense of glamorous realism that truly distinguishes the pageantry of ballroom from more theatrical or satirical forms of drag. "I learned to soften my features in ballroom. I started out walking in the 'butch queen up in drag' category, but as I've started my transition, I'm moving toward the 'femme queen' categories. That requires me to use even less makeup because I'm showing them woman."

The preference for realism or "realness" sometimes extends to Calypso being required to remove her warpaint altogether. "Sometimes the judges ask to see more 'washed face' to see what your features were like before you applied makeup," she explains, "because I can create a cheekbone, but they want to know if I *have* the cheekbones before I apply makeup. In ballroom, the makeup is more of an enhancer rather than something you stick on top."

"It takes me 30 to 40 minutes to do my makeup," she reveals. "One thing I like to do first is prime and moisturize. I also fill in the creases and smile lines with primer and translucent setting powder, and then I let that sit for a while before I apply my base. I also use Blue Marble setting spray. If you use that, you will be good for the rest of the night. You can take a shower with your makeup on and your face will not come off."

Calypso applies equal attention to detail when it comes to her sartorial choices. "I love a good leotard," she confesses. "It's great for dance, but I always try to do stuff with a leotard look that's out of the box. I have an overactive imagination, so a lot of my looks for drag shows are extremely cartoony, but with a high-fashion twist. I had a bumblebee outfit made that is all black and gold sequins with wings on it, so when I do a Beyoncé number, people can see that I am literally the queen bee."

"I'm inspired by a lot of classic ballroom fashion and I love showing off my body," she admits, "so I like anything that exposes the hips and legs. As a dancer, I love anything that is stoned or fringed. I do a lot of crazy spins and moves in the air, so it always gives that added element of movement, which is really effective."

Despite her ambitious fashions, Calypso emphasizes the importance of creativity over budget. "I grew up with my grandparents and we didn't have a lot of money, so anything I wanted, I would have to make myself," Calypso reveals. "When I was in school, I was really into dance, so I was always in the house hand sewing or hot glueing. My grandma made hats, so I got used to making the things that I wanted."

"I was also obsessed with cartoons and *Pokémon* and *Yu-Gi-Oh!*, and through those characters I was inspired to create costumes for Halloween and for dance shows. I still do that, because I like to tell stories with my performances. I believe it's a lot easier to snatch people's attention with a story than by just getting up and twerking for an entire song."

Calypso continues to take inspiration from pop-culture icons and has a well-known Catwoman routine. "I also do a Harley Quinn number. I start off in a straightjacket inside a body bag, and somebody will carry me out and throw me onto the stage. I then unzip the body bag from the inside and start lip-syncing to a slow track. Next, I perform being electrocuted, then the track mixes up with house beats and speeds up, and suddenly I'm giving the audience vogueing, spins and dips, and things get really chaotic, and I'm flipping and swinging from the ceiling. I slide under tables, jump on people, and roll around like I'm trying to escape an asylum. It's a full production."

"IT'S A LOT EASIER TO SNATCH PEOPLE'S ATTENTION WITH A STORY THAN BY JUST GETTING UP AND TWERKING."

"Musically, I'm inspired by Beyoncé, who I also impersonate," she continues. "My go-to tracks when performing at drag shows are 'Crazy In Love' (the live Vegas version), 'Work This Pussy' by Tiana Taylor, or anything by FKA Twigs or Janelle Monae. I also love jazz samples mixed with house beats. I love to play with musicality and show the audience different things to every beat of the music."

Calypso navigates different gender presentations, moving from natural to high drag femininity, and performs in multiple arenas, including ballroom pageants, TV shows, dance, drag, and cabaret performances—all while managing her own transition journey and hardly appearing to break a sweat. "I consider my drag to be universal," she proclaims. "I can apply my drag not only to ballroom but also to drag shows, to the art of vogueing, for television. I can still be Calypso, but I bend the makeup and style of performance to whichever scene I'm working in."

Professional to a T, Calypso also believes that entertainers should be rewarded based on merit and hard work. "Artists' pay shouldn't be based purely on their visibility or how much publicity they have. There are plenty of girls out there who don't make it on TV but work just as hard, are just as creative, and perform just as many numbers in a night."

Her pet peeve? "I see a lot of queens on stage attempting a death drop—what we in ballroom would call a dip—but they just fall flat on their back. The true secret to a dip is that you never land straight on your back. The idea is that you are moving so fast that you *appear* to land flat. In reality, your leg is sliding out and at the same time your hands are sliding out, so regardless of whether you're spinning or up in the air, it's a slide procedure rather than a jump and a slap. If a queen does it and you can hear the impact, she's not doing it right. It's all about the illusion of falling."

So what's next for Calypso? "More than anything, I want to get out of the country and perform all over the world," she reveals. "Taiwan, Japan, the UK, France, and Italy—they do a lot of balls in Paris and Milan. I wanna go out there and have the opportunity to walk in ballroom in Europe."

As Calypso embarks on the next phase of her career, she has valuable words of encouragement for those who are just starting out. "My main advice is just to stay true to yourself. I would say that to anyone starting out. Stay true, have fun, and don't beat yourself up. When I first started, I was trying so hard to be like everyone else and to score perfect 10s, and I was so hard on myself. If I worked more diligently, and was more true to my own journey, and didn't try to do my makeup like this person, or dance like that person, I would be here twice as fast."

"I may mix different looks and performance styles, but one thing never changes: I am a woman."

60 SECONDS WITH CALYPSO

DESCRIBE YOURSELF IN THREE WORDS

Spontaneous. Seductive. Show-stopping.

WHERE IS YOUR SPIRITUAL HOME?

My mind. There, I can do/be whatever I want without any consequences.

WHAT WOULD YOU NEVER LEAVE THE HOUSE WITHOUT?

My bag. It's where I keep all my snacks!

HOW DO YOU HANDLE A CRISIS?

I take a step back and evaluate the situation very logically. I get all the details first.

WHAT IS SOMETHING NOT MANY PEOPLE KNOW ABOUT YOU?

I donate my time and sometimes even my belongings to LGBTQ+ folks in need when I can.

IF YOU RULED THE WORLD FOR A DAY, WHAT CHANGE WOULD YOU MAKE?

I would order that everyone must bathe at least once per day.

IN BED WITH

CRYSTAL

Equal parts sex kitten and comic-book super villain, Crystal has been whipping the cool kids of East London into a frenzy for years with her wild circus-heavy drag revues. She is best known for her androgynous, fetish-inspired fashion aesthetic; her death-defying aerial stunts; and for breaking into the mainstream as a fierce competitor in the first season of *RuPaul's Drag Race UK*. Pull up a pillow and join Crystal as she spills the tea on her hopes, heroines, and hanging upside down.

"She-Ra meets Harley Quinn meets Barbarella. This was my entrance look for *Drag Race UK*, and I'm wearing a gorgeous sculptural piece by Colin Horgan."

"If Cecil Beaton and Leigh Bowery had an overconfident baby."

"My name was inspired by lots of little things that all came together at once," says Crystal. "Before drag, I was working in a corporate role for a crystal jeweler. It was the most strait-laced environment imaginable. I had to wear a suit and really tone down my personality, which was weird, because I was working in the most camp place in the world and I had to be the least camp I'd ever been in my entire life."

Ultimately, though, the world of luxury goods couldn't keep Crystal clean cut for long, and she had to escape the corporate rat race. "So Crystal is partly a rebellion against that heteronormative world," she explains, "because I felt so buttoned down there. Literally!"

Her name, much like the gemstone, is multifaceted. Crystal was also a nickname affectionately bestowed on her by childhood "theater geek" friends due to her love of all things glitz and glam. "I've always been obsessed with crystals, because they're dazzling, ostentatious, and cheap," she says, "just like me."

The path to drag superstardom, however, was never cut with laser precision. "Crystal came into being accidentally," she confesses. "I was producing variety cabaret shows, in addition to my day job, and appearing primarily as a circus performer. I loved booking drag queens and I realized that it looked like a lot of fun and could help take my aerial routines into new and exciting venues."

In her grand stage debut, Crystal appeared in costume as the Diva Plavalaguna, the statuesque blue-skinned alien soprano from intergalactic action thriller *The Fifth Element*. As entrances go, it was anything but subtle. "I had [punk drag legend] Baby Lame dressed as Milla Jovovich hidden underneath an enormous blue skirt, which also housed all these long, pendulous tentacles," she says. "During the operatic section of the lip-sync, Baby appeared and bit them all open, spraying blue goo absolutely everywhere!"

Science fiction has remained a consistent source of inspiration for Crystal's work as she's developed. "I'm inspired by sci-fi and fantasy babes," she says. "Those hyper-sexualized comic-book-style women of the '80s and '90s like Daryl Hannah in *Blade Runner* or Poison Ivy. That's the type of woman I might have seen as a kid and thought, 'Oh my god! That woman is living her fiercest and most fully realized self and she is in fucking control. And with superpowers!'"

Like many queens, Crystal is heavily influenced by the female icons she grew up on. "That probably came from feeling repressed," she muses. "When I was a kid, between the ages of six and 12, I grew up in a really rural part of Canada. I was very much the only gay in the village, even though I was a bit too young to know I was gay. You know when you're different, don't you? So to me, those badass women were like a window into radical self-expression."

Music was another crucial outlet that allowed Crystal to discover her inner style rebel. "Crystal is a little bit punky, a little bit sexy, and just a little bit desperate," she says. "I love the gender-bending new wave musicians of the 1980s like Siouxsie and the Banshees, Blondie, and the iconic David Bowie."

Icons of androgyny are present in everything Crystal does. While many contemporary queens are cinched, padded, and tucked to within an inch of their life, Crystal prefers to let it all hang out. "I think I'm a little more willing to play with gender than other mainstream drag queens," she explains. "I'm not quite so concerned with the idea of female illusion, which I think many people assume is the objective of all drag. I'm just trying to express myself and create a character, and you can interpret that as whatever gender you want."

So how long does it take to create that character? "The total transformation takes about three hours," she reveals. "The first two hours are makeup and after that it's an hour on hair, costume, corsetry, tights, and that sort of stuff. I normally start to feel myself when the lashes go on. Then, all of a sudden, I'm like, 'OH!' and instantly there's an entirely different energy in the room."

Even when showcasing a cheeky plume of chest hair, Crystal is undeniably snatched for the gods. Her face is a blend of misty colors, sharp angles, and perfectly placed jewels. "My signature makeup look usually includes two sparkling crystal dots under my eyes and *very* extreme 1980s blush," she says. "I like to try different things with the rest of my face each time I get ready, as long as the makeup looks a bit mean. I think that's very much a signature for Crystal. I still *hate* drawing on eyebrows though."

So what does Crystal wish she knew about beating her mug when she started out? "Even though I probably should have, I didn't realize how busted I looked in

"I NORMALLY START TO FEEL MYSELF WHEN THE LASHES GO ON. THEN, ALL OF A SUDDEN, I'M LIKE, 'OH!' AND INSTANTLY THERE'S AN ENTIRELY DIFFERENT ENERGY IN THE ROOM."

the early years. We queens always tend to think we look amazing, which is the only reason we leave the house."

For a long time, busted drag was all she knew. "My first experience of drag was seeing a really terrible show at the one gay bar in my hometown in Canada," she recalls. "I just thought drag was really old-fashioned until I moved to the UK and fell into the East London scene."

That scene was the site of a massive cabaret renaissance in the 2010s, with venues like Dalston Superstore, The Glory, and Bethnal Green Working Men's Club showcasing wild and wacky drag shows that were a far cry from the Shirley Bassey impersonators who had dominated Soho for decades. It was here that Crystal started to take shape.

"East London drag is really based in clubbing culture," she explains. "So you've got infamous club hosts, fashion queens, and drag go-go dancers who are all these fabulous yet unhinged creatures of the night. They'll always be the last ones at the party and they can be rolling around on the floor with one eyelash hanging off and still be the most glamorous and exciting people in the room."

As she began to make a name for herself on the circuit, Crystal realized she had stumbled upon something she could really stick to. "There was no plan," she admits. "I have never had a plan. I've fallen from one thing to the next my whole life. But drag is the first thing that has captured my attention, because it's so different all the time. I'm lucky enough with my platform that my drag doesn't have to be just one thing. It exists in many mediums, so I can always try new challenges and I love the variety."

For Crystal, the perks of the gig are obvious. "I get to come up with absolutely ridiculous concepts and live them out in the club for the adoration of scores of fans," she exclaims. "And it's such a privilege to live out your little gay boy fantasies on stage and get paid for it. It's also amazing being your own boss and having the power to say no to things. I'm not answerable to anyone."

"I'VE FALLEN FROM ONE THING TO THE NEXT MY WHOLE LIFE. BUT DRAG IS THE FIRST THING THAT HAS CAPTURED MY ATTENTION, BECAUSE IT'S SO DIFFERENT ALL THE TIME. DRAG DOESN'T HAVE TO BE JUST ONE THING. IT EXISTS IN MANY MEDIUMS."

Not one to rest on her laurels, Crystal is always looking toward the next big goal. "I'm aiming for world domination, with an emphasis on *domination!*" she teases. "I've been working on a show where I want to enter from the ceiling, hanging from a giant crystal chandelier that I can perform aerial circus tricks on."

If money were no object, what show-stopping look would she want to wear on the red carpet? "I'd love to be hatched from a giant crystal egg," she says. "Or enter in a glass coffin like Snow White and then emerge in a suit of armor made entirely from cut glass. That would be camp!"

As much as her star has risen, Crystal still feels her roots are firmly planted in the scene that birthed her. "The LGBTQ+ community is fully intrinsic to what I do," she stresses. "I would not have a career without them, and they are still the people I want to impress the most. Even though I may have broken the mainstream to some degree, the tastemakers will always be the East London queers."

Crystal also remains passionate about promoting other artists, and her own productions invariably showcase a range of bodies and identities. "Many of the performers I work with in the drag community are not cisgender men," she explains. "They're cis women and trans women and men and nonbinary and gender-fluid people. They're still giving the best shows out there and are some of the best performers I know. There should be no limits on who can perform drag. That diversity is really present on the local scenes, and I think that needs to be represented a lot more in the global mainstream."

Like all great comic-book icons, Crystal believes that great power comes with great responsibility. "Anyone who is lucky enough to have a platform has a responsibility to create positive change," she says. "Even if that's just in a small and entertaining way. I think we at least have an obligation to speak out against the restrictions of the gender binary and the issues facing women and trans people. But at our best, we should also be at the forefront of political change. I try to do that with my drag."

"Crystal has really taught me to embrace my sexuality and camp power," she says, reflecting on her personal journey as an artist. "Those are things that have been weaponized against queer people, but Crystal has taught me to turn that weapon back on the world. She has also taught me, when in doubt, climb something and hump it!"

And what about her advice to those who would love to follow in her footsteps? "Don't!" she jokes. "Drag is full. It's one in, one out. You'll have to wait for me to die! But seriously, if you're looking to get into drag, think about what you're trying to express and why. Don't just copy or emulate what you see on TV or online, because then the world of drag becomes a snake eating its own tail. Look at your favorite films, comics, books, or old fashion magazines. Look for references outside of drag. Think about what excites you, and then use drag to tell that story."

"Be gay. Spray paint your name on a warehouse.

"DON'T JUST COPY OR EMULATE WHAT YOU SEE ON TV OR ONLINE ... THINK ABOUT WHAT EXCITES YOU, AND THEN USE DRAG TO TELL THAT STORY."

60 SECONDS WITH CRYSTAL

DESCRIBE YOURSELF IN THREE WORDS

Sparkly. Cheap. Transparent.

WHERE IS YOUR SPIRITUAL HOME?

A Las Vegas strip club.

WHAT IS YOUR FAIL-SAFE PARTY TRICK?

Climb something and gyrate!

WHAT WOULD YOU NEVER LEAVE THE HOUSE WITHOUT?

Self-delusion.

HOW DO YOU HANDLE A CRISIS?

Binge drink.

WHAT IS SOMETHING NOT MANY PEOPLE KNOW ABOUT YOU?

I can fit my entire fist in my mouth.

IF YOU RULED THE WORLD FOR A DAY, WHAT CHANGE WOULD YOU MAKE?

Outlaw billionaires and distribute a global living wage.

SLAYING THE HOUSE DOWN WITH

TYNOMI BANKS

Tynomi Banks is a veteran of drag and a tightly choreographed whirlwind of a performer. Her style combines catwalk queen with pop diva to create a fiery, show-stopping persona that's impossible to ignore. Most recently, she was announced as a contestant on the inaugural Canadian edition of *RuPaul's Drag Race*. So sit tight, buckle up, and watch out for flying lace fronts as Tynomi explains what drag means to her and why you absolutely can teach an old dog new tricks.

"I may have not won the statue ... that's because I AM the statue—a 100-karat-gold statue! Styled by Marc Andrew Smith."

"I can remember the first time I ever saw drag," Tynomi says. "I'm a little bit of a nerd when it comes to comic books and I was watching a lot of *X-Men* at the time, which I love because they tackle real issues but in a fantasy world. Mutants for me are a metaphor for queer people and people of color, so I really related to them a lot. Anyway, I snuck out of school to go to a club. I was living on campus and not out to my friends at the time, so I just made a gay friend and we got in the car and drove downtown."

What Tynomi experienced when she hit her destination was a world away from anything she had known before. "When I got to this club, it was a crazy experience," she admits. "I felt like the scene in *Queer as Folk* where the kid goes to a gay bar for the first time. Music was blaring and there were half-naked boys everywhere. All of a sudden, the lights went down and a spotlight came up on a door with the X-Men logo on it. A queen named Sofonda Cox emerged in a cloud of smoke dressed as Storm with her hair flying around, and I had this sense where I was no longer nervous and everyone in that club was together in the moment of her performance."

It was a few more years before Tynomi would dip her own toe into the waters of drag. "I was always dancing as a hobby and I wanted to pursue that more, but I came from a very strict Jamaican Christian background," she reveals. "My family wanted me to go to school and not one for the arts, but they didn't mind me pursuing dance as a hobby."

Tynomi moved downtown when she was 21 and promptly joined a dance group. "I did shows and music videos, but I never planned on doing drag until I tried it," she insists. "There are two times when drag queens are born, and they are Pride and Halloween. I'm a Halloween baby. I did it twice for Halloween, and there's an overwhelming feeling of power you get when you step into your own character like you're an undercover agent. Everyone wanted pictures with me, so I felt like a celebrity. My feet hurt so badly at the end of the night and my toes were mangled, but it was worth it."

Around two years later, a good friend was organizing a show and needed an extra drag queen who could dance. Cue Tynomi. "It was me and two other queens named Heavenly Heights and Divine Darling, and we formed a group called Girls Gone Wild," she recalls. "We began to perform every Wednesday at a club called The Barn. We put on amazing dance shows each week and we did that for two or three years until the place closed."

"Morticia Addams x black girl magic. Styled by Marc Andrew Smith."

Deeply unhappy in the job she was in at the time, Tynomi began to see drag as her ticket out of the corporate rigmarole. "I was in event planning for a company that closed down, and so I worked as a coordinator at a hotel, and that was not my tea, it was not fun," she cringes. "There was a whole year where the work really affected me and I was not in a good head space, because the nine-to-five life was just not my vibe. So I stuck with dancing, but then that stemmed out into performing more drag. What I wanted was to be my own celebrity, I guess. Then in around 2006, I really started to take drag to the next level."

Tynomi's distinctive brand references major pop-culture icons. "I would describe Tynomi as the love child of Tyra Banks and Naomi Campbell with the fire of Beyoncé," she explains, referring to the way in which she has handpicked qualities from the divas to create a completely unique stage persona. "I loved Tyra Banks [in *America's Next Top Model*], but she also had a crazy side to her which was kind of cuckoo. Then there was Naomi Campbell, who's just That Bitch. She's stubborn as hell and knows her shit."

When she started performing in drag, it was not widely seen as a valid career choice and came at a personal cost. "Even getting to know somebody romantically was hard, because nobody wanted to date a drag queen," she admits. "They think we party way too much, have irregular schedules, and do drugs. With *RuPaul's Drag Race* came knowledge, so the public got to meet these contestants, hear their stories, and see them as human. That opened up the conversation in a way that's been really successful for the younger generation."

Now that she's graduating toward veteran class, Tynomi has been forthcoming in her support of newer performers. "I've become friends with young people who literally started drag secretly in their bedrooms," she says. "I have friends who have been kicked out of their homes because their families don't agree with it, but then drag has helped to channel their life in a new direction. So you get these stunning young queens who don't have any performing ability, but you can teach that. Toronto has the largest community for drag because of that. Everybody here wants to be a queen now and everyone is very supportive of that."

Having had to work so hard to prove the validity of her career choice, Tynomi has bittersweet feelings toward the swathes of openly queer kids flocking to drag today. "Obviously, I'm shady sometimes," she laughs. "I'm like, 'Bitch, stay in your lane.' It doesn't happen all the time, but it took a moment to accept that this was happening. I think what's important is to respect the people who came before you, because your elders have stories. This generation is very ambitious and focused on trends, and that's something I need to keep up with, so we can both learn from each other. As long as you have a positive attitude, you can go a long way."

Tynomi admits to getting very nervous before a show but insists that simply taking her time on her preshow routine calms her more than any relaxation technique. "If I'm really nervous, I'll literally take a spa-type shower, do a facial shave, and take my time to lotion and pamper," she explains. "I always listen to music that I won't be performing, and that really helps calm me down. The quickest face I can do takes around 45 minutes, but I hate being rushed. An hour and a half is perfect."

While she's retained something of a signature style, Tynomi's makeup has changed a lot over the nearly two decades she's been on top, and she's open to what she can learn from other artists. "I like updating my face," she says. "There was a point around two years ago that I felt I had had the same face for so long, and I wanted to learn new techniques from different people. I never went to school for makeup; I was taught by my drag mother. I never watched any tutorials. So I invited a few queens whose makeup I admired over to mine and we would do a regular girls' night. They would teach me new techniques, and I started making notes."

"I describe my makeup station as a war zone," she jokes. "When I do my face, I feel like a crazy person until the moment I dust the powder off at the end. I use highlight and setting powder all over; it looks like I've been attacked with flour. Then I take my nice beauty brush and sweep it all off right at the end, and then it's perfect. I've never got tired of that final reveal moment of looking crazy and then looking amazing!"

She's renowned for her signature hair toss, so what does Tynomi do to keep her silken tresses stuck firmly on her head? "I'm lucky that my head is not too big and not too small, so wigs tend to lay perfectly on my head," she explains. "Most wigs have clips on the inside that I can clip into my hair, but some also have elastic, so even when I shave my head, I can secure it like a baseball cap. I then use spirit gum on the soft lace so it stays stuck flat to my head. I glue across the forehead and around the temples and over the ear. That means I can be all crazy and get down without my hair flying off."

"I'VE NEVER GOT TIRED OF THAT FINAL REVEAL MOMENT OF LOOKING CRAZY AND THEN LOOKING AMAZING!"

On one occasion, however, Tynomi was performing at a bar in Toronto and got a little carried away. "I remember I was whipping my hair around and the crowd was screaming for me and my wig just flew off into the distance," she howls. "Luckily I have a nice-shaped head, so I made the decision just to own that moment and go even harder with my routine. People were actually screaming louder and throwing more money."

Ultimately, Tynomi believes that failures are more important than triumphs in defining long-term success. "I think you have to make mistakes, because that's the only way to get better at what you're doing," she ventures. "It's also really important to ask questions. Online tutorials can be useful, but in real life, there is a person right beside you. Reach out and see what you can learn from people. Also, not everyone is naturally talented at everything, and it's important to realize that. You could be a great makeup artist and you can make a living from that, but when it comes to performance, some people just don't get it. Nowadays, everyone wants to be on the stage, but don't get frustrated if it doesn't come naturally … just know what you're capable of. Try things out, of course, but drag skills can take you in many different directions."

"I THINK YOU HAVE TO MAKE MISTAKES, BECAUSE THAT'S THE ONLY WAY TO GET BETTER AT WHAT YOU'RE DOING."

So what path did drag have in mind for Tynomi? "Drag saved my life," she says. "I found drag when I had no direction and I didn't know where I was going, and it helped me communicate in a different way. Drag helped me figure out my frustration and a lot of my anger. In that way, it's like my therapy. I could be so sad that I'm crying, and then I could decide, 'Okay, I'm going to get in drag today.' Honest to god, the moment I put on a face, my mood changes. It's a lifesaver. It helps. That's what drag is to me."

"Channeling modern-day Whitney Houston and feeling gorgeous. Styled by Marc Andrew Smith."

60 SECONDS
WITH TYNOMI

DESCRIBE YOURSELF IN THREE WORDS
Confident. Fun. Sexy.

WHERE IS YOUR SPIRITUAL HOME?
On stage, where I feel most connected to life.

WHAT IS YOUR FAIL-SAFE PARTY TRICK?
To ghost it by leaving and creating my own atmosphere at home. I want to be in control.

WHAT WOULD YOU NEVER LEAVE THE HOUSE WITHOUT?
My clutch, which includes everything in a drag queen's emergency kit.

HOW DO YOU HANDLE A CRISIS?
By listening and reminding myself to stay calm.

WHAT IS SOMETHING NOT MANY PEOPLE KNOW ABOUT YOU?
I can eat a WHOLE cheesecake by myself.

IF YOU RULED THE WORLD FOR A DAY, WHAT CHANGE WOULD YOU MAKE?
I'd make it a safe place for everyone.

Striking Beauties and High-

GLAM

Concept-Look Queens

From golden-age glamazons to the avant garde, these elegant and sartorial creatures could be lifted straight out of a high-fashion editorial spread. They have style, they have grace, and they sure do serve a lot of face! Prepare to be dazzled by the groundbreaking art of the glam brigade.

COLORING IN WITH

ART SIMONE

Aussie legend Art Simone is the class president of antipodean beauty icons. She is akin to a Type A prom queen, seemingly transported from a universe comprised only of glitter and smiles. Having experimented with cosmetics from a young age, she has created some of the most followed and respected drag makeup channels on the internet and has gone on to tour the world and collaborate with major beauty brands. Next on the list, world domination!

Art Simone at Austin International Drag Festival 2019.

"My first exposure to drag was *The Rocky Horror Picture Show*," Art remembers, "which I was adamant that I would really dislike, but my mom made me watch it and then bought me tickets to see it as a live stage show, and I walked out of there like, 'Oh my god, these are my people!' So that's my first big memory of the idea of drag. I was already into makeup and horror movies and I was creating all of these characters in my bedroom, transforming myself with makeup, but I hadn't really pushed into the drag side of it just yet."

Art landed straight As throughout high school and garnered the titles of debate captain, drama captain, and music captain. "I was an overachiever," she understates. "In high school, I did anything I could to keep myself busy and avoid sports. I picked up every extracurricular activity that I could. I think I was lucky to have a good enough experience in high school, compared to some of the horror stories I hear. Most people were scared of me because they thought I was weird, but they usually left me alone. Looking back, I was definitely the leader of the misfits. We had this weird group of the strangest people you could throw together, but it worked."

Art Simone is colorful, camp, kooky, and high concept. "I play on the line between what I would consider commercial drag and artistic drag," she explains. "I started out way left of center being really alternative and doing performance art covering myself in blood, but as I've worked more over the years, I've had to clean up my image. I like to be the representation in the mainstream for our community and for all the kids out there because I didn't really have that to look up to growing up. I didn't see drag queens on TV, so that's something I've been pushing to do. So I look at the things I have done—movies, commercials, and online campaigns—and I see that commerciality as a positive instead of selling out. Now I've had those platforms, it allows me to spread some joy and color to the masses, which I think is a great thing."

Spreading joy is exactly what Art does every year at Broken Heel Festival, a fabulous three-day festival that celebrates the camp theatrics of *Priscilla, Queen of the Desert* in its spiritual home of New South Wales. "One of the things I really pride myself on is taking drag to regional places in Australia," she says. "I run drag nights in four venues in regional Victoria where there aren't many gay bars or drag shows, and I get to bring them a bit of fabulousness every week. One of the towns we work in was previously Australia's most homophobic town."

When it comes to thinking up new looks and performances, Art advises keeping an open mind and an open eye at all times. "I find inspiration in everything and anything," she reveals. "I just get a weird idea and I run with it. I used to get inspired by walking through a $2 shop and seeing something weird and thinking I could make a fabulous headpiece out of it. Sometimes I'm really lucky in that I get to work with other artists, and maybe I've created a wig and I can tell them that's my starting point for a design."

Art cut her performing teeth at Dracula's Cabaret, a theater restaurant with venues in Melbourne and Queensland. "I started working there as soon as I turned 18 and finished high school, so I went straight into doing five or six nights of drag a week," she remembers. "And at Dracula's I could look however I wanted to every single night. In fact, they encouraged it. It became this competition, like a game with myself. I would do all red, all blue, cover myself in 10,000 eyeballs ... That's where I started to get the motivation to do these creative looks. Unfortunately, you can't show up to Sally's hen party bright yellow with glitter snot coming out of your nose, so I've had to channel my creativity into more fabulous headpieces."

The persona Art Simone has cultivated is bubbly, ebullient, and overflowing with brightly colored energy. "I'm a bit of an Ocker," she laughs. "I'm not sure how many people know that word ... Ocker is someone who is really rigid, a true Aussie bloke. Like Crocodile Dundee. People have said to me before, 'I just want to be your friend!' Which is such a nice thing to say. I'm just a loud and heightened version of myself. When I first started doing drag, I didn't realize at the time, but all my performances were quite selfish because they were all about how I felt and what I wanted to put on the stage. I didn't care too much what anybody else wanted to see. It was very much about expressing myself because I felt a certain way and needed to get it off my chest. Now I've developed by learning that you have a much better time if the crowd is on your side, so I'm definitely something of a people pleaser. Now when I put stuff together, I think about what the audience expects and what will put them in a good mood."

Art is probably best known for her impossibly snatched mug, often featuring razor-sharp almond eyes and eyebrows on fleek. "My eyeliner always stays the same, but my eyebrows are different every single day," she explains. "I hate doing brows, and it's the thing I'm most self-conscious about. I did a brand collaboration with an eyebrow product and I remember getting to the studio to shoot and panicking because there were 12 people watching me apply my eyebrows. I've got terrible eyesight and I'm legally blind in my left eye, so I have to do my makeup with a mirror right in my face."

Her top tip for achieving such a polished look is to simply take your time over it. "My whole face can take 2–4 hours," she confesses. "I have to stop after every step and take photos of my face and review those to see if it's wonky. It takes me a really long time, but I enjoy that time. I get into my zone and listen to music or put a TV show I have watched a thousand times on in the background."

When it comes to red carpet fashions, Art doesn't scrimp on ambition. "My dream look would be to wear some kind of digital projector with face-mapping technology so I could change my makeup," she reveals. "I saw Lady Gaga do a similar thing once. She did a David Bowie tribute where she was stood on stage and Bowie's makeup was projected onto her. I would love to do the same thing but with a portable projector that also works on the dress. I'd love one of those amazing high-tech outfits that have LED elements running throughout so that I could change my look as I walked down the red carpet. I'm so indecisive that I would just want my dream look to be a thousand looks at once."

As for obstacles, Art's primary nemesis is her inner saboteur. "I am my own biggest enemy," she admits. "I am way too hard on myself. I get stressed aiming for perfection and never being able to achieve it. That's the thing that freaks me out more than anything. Sometimes I wonder why I didn't just go out there on my first show with a cigarette hanging out the corner of my mouth and say, 'Alright c***s!' Because maybe then people would just be happy to see me show up. But I think my biggest stress is trying to maintain the standard I've set for myself. I'm a Virgo. I don't know what that means, but I've been told that's why I'm like this."

Art believes you should only do drag if you're enjoying yourself and it's a pleasurable experience. Then practice, practice, practice! "I think since *Drag Race* came along, people have been brainwashed into believing everyone has a drag house and a drag mother, but that's not how it works for most people," she points out. "If you want to do drag, just go and fucking do it. Don't ever wait for anyone to give you anything. Go online, watch some videos, buy some glitter, and have fun with it. You've got to be doing it for the right reason and not just because you want to get famous quickly."

"I AM MY OWN BIGGEST ENEMY ... I AM WAY TOO HARD ON MYSELF. I GET STRESSED AIMING FOR PERFECTION AND NEVER BEING ABLE TO ACHIEVE IT."

Despite her captivating looks, Art is reluctant to get up on a soap box. "I've always seen myself to be a distraction from what's happening in the real world, so I have never consciously made my drag political," she explains. "The only time I did use my voice in that way was when we had the plebiscite [referendum] in Australia. They asked Australians whether same-sex couples should have the right to marry, and it was a horrendous time for the LGBTQ population because it was an optional vote."

"I was doing regional shows in Victoria and explaining the vote to the people enjoying our shows every week. I said, 'You may look at this postal vote and think it doesn't really affect us, or you may forget about it and throw it in the bin, but please know that this piece of paper affects our livelihoods, and if you enjoy what we do each week, please support us in this.'"

Art is a consummate professional and the living embodiment of steely showbiz determination. "Whenever I arrive at a gig, I always say hi to the organizers first, ask if they have a sound system, and make sure everything is alright," she says. "At one gig, I checked and they said everything was fine and then they literally had a tiny Bluetooth speaker for a room with 200 people. It turned out they had tested the sound in an empty room. When it came to my performance, I had someone stand behind me and walk this tiny speaker around the room while I was performing, and people could hear my lips smacking and my jewelry clanging around."

Like any drag queen worth her salt, Art has had to get ready in some questionable spaces. "I did one show where the dressing room was a bathroom," she recalls, "which is fine, but then halfway through this show, I suddenly realized there was a person who had passed out in a cubicle and I just started screaming. I couldn't believe that nobody had seen them when they were preparing the space for us."

Art knows to expect the unexpected in drag, but she is more than capable of rolling with the punches, whatever the season. "There are so many moments in my life where I've been like, 'What the fuck is my job?' Because people just love to put drag queens where they don't belong. There was one Christmas where they'd replaced Santa Claus with me, in the biggest shopping district in Melbourne. They put me there, at the peak of summer, every Saturday and Sunday throughout December. I was in the back of a convertible wearing fur and lip-syncing 'All I Want For Christmas Is You.' It was unbearable. There are so many strange things I've done, but I love each and every one of them."

60 SECONDS WITH ART

DESCRIBE YOURSELF IN THREE WORDS

Ocker. Technicolor. Effervescent.

WHERE IS YOUR SPIRITUAL HOME?

Melbourne, Australia.

WHAT IS YOUR FAIL-SAFE PARTY TRICK?

My giant mouth.

WHAT WOULD YOU NEVER LEAVE THE HOUSE WITHOUT?

Superglue.

HOW DO YOU HANDLE A CRISIS?

By keeping myself busy.

WHAT IS SOMETHING NOT MANY PEOPLE KNOW ABOUT YOU?

I have a third nipple.

IF YOU RULED THE WORLD FOR A DAY, WHAT CHANGE WOULD YOU MAKE?

I'd stop Australia being region-blocked from viewing all the exciting new entertainment being produced overseas.

RIDING THE TRAIN WITH

SUM ING WONG

The unshakable Sum Ting Wong is the radiant, social media–savvy chanteuse with the voice of an angel and the mouth of a sailor. She is most at home belting out pop hits and indie classics, and she paints her face in stunning, shimmering strokes. So hop on board for a few stops and get a handle on where she's coming from (and where she's going)!

"A modern interpretation of Asian imperial royalty for the *Drag Race UK* finale. The kimono-esque dress is made with hand-sewn silk and velvet with diamanté crystals and was created by David Henson."

"If Moana and Mulan had a baby, it would be this outfit. Inspired by cherry blossoms but with a tropical twist, it was my entrance look for *Drag Race UK*, created by myself."

"Sum Ting Wong was born in 2015," she reveals. "My housemate was on a television show called *Drag Queens of London*, and I always had to help him with his makeup. And then I thought, 'actually, do you know what? I could do this way better than you!' And so I entered Drag Idol UK, the largest drag competition in the country, placed third, and I've been a drag queen ever since."

Sum Ting has always been confident and able to turn her hand to different things. "I was a very annoying kid," she admits. "My dad has a video where I'm telling him off for pronouncing 'safari park' wrong in his Vietnamese accent. But I told him off in this thick Brummie accent, and a Brummie person trying to lecture anyone on pronunciation is inherently hilarious. So I was that annoying little kid, but very creative."

"I played a lot of sports, so I was never bullied at school," she notes. "But music was my main passion. I played piano and guitar. I grew up listening to R&B, emo, and pop punk. It was a very weird mix. I would listen to Linkin Park followed by Destiny's Child. I think that's all come together in the music I'm making now."

Sum Ting's musical inclinations eventually proved to be the perfect background for a career in drag. "I absolutely love drag because it was an avenue for me to sing and not be scared of it," she exclaims. "In the past, I was in bands and sang at open mics but never had aspirations of being a professional singer. Suddenly, ever since I started singing in drag, I get to make a living from it."

On drag's magic power to help her sing, Sum Ting says, "It's a bit of a mask. And it literally is a mask because I'm wearing about five kilos [pounds] of makeup at a time. And then you get to take it off like a backward superhero, and that's the part I like the most. I enjoy being inconspicuous and unknown like Clark Kent."

Sum Ting is particularly skilled at creating masks and can take inspiration from even the most humdrum of sources. "Makeup came to me fairly easy because I always drew and painted," she reflects, "so it's just applying that skill but on a different canvas. You trade in paper for skin, and you get all these fancy brushes that are unfortunately seven times more expensive than paint brushes."

"The look side of things comes from the mundane. My signature makeup look is a woman popping to the shops. If I look out of place because of my makeup, I've done something wrong. I want to look out of place because I'm a 6'1" man in heels!"

So how long does it take to prepare to go out for some milk? "It can be anywhere from half an hour to four hours," she reveals. "I don't need to cover my eyebrows because I shave them into the shape I want. I no longer color correct because my foundation is quite orange anyway, but I used to use an orange foundation under my base shade to cancel out the blue tones in my beard area. When it comes to my eyes, I basically color the shapes around my natural eye. My makeup is very simple. I'll just pop some color in the crease and I'm ready."

So what's her advice for aspiring drag makeup wizards? "I think as long as you don't look totally stupid, it's okay," she reasons, "and if stupid is the look you're going for, then that's also fine. Everything in art is really subjective, so you should do whatever you want with your face, and if you have the conviction to carry it off, then that's fine."

In order to conquer drag, Sum Ting had to leave behind a high-rolling marketing career in the city. "I was an office wanker," she confesses. "That's what I like to call it because you either are one or you aren't. I hated it with a passion. I hated every single bit of it. I was working in marketing, but I could have been doing anything because it was basically a job that could be done by a computer. I think most jobs will be like that eventually."

"I was originally doing drag alongside work, and it was very draining, mundane, and a bit of a mind rot," she admits. "It got to a point where a venue called and asked me to cover a show that night because someone had dropped out. I said no because I was at work. Then I hung up the phone, sat there, and realized I could make more money working full time in drag. I quit my job there and then, did the gig, and never went back to an office again."

It was a move that paid off when Sum Ting Wong was announced as one of the inaugural queens on the first season of *RuPaul's Drag Race UK*, propelling her to international stardom overnight. While the pressures of fame might prove overwhelming for some, Sum Ting takes them in her considerable stride.

"If anything, I think I can get away with more now," she reveals. "It's weird because I should have to be more perfect and more amazing, but the fan base is just so happy to see you. Sometimes I feel like I could just go on stage and fart and they would still cheer. It's utterly bizarre. The less I do, the more they cheer. But the best

"EVERYTHING IN ART IS REALLY SUBJECTIVE, SO YOU SHOULD DO WHATEVER YOU WANT WITH YOUR FACE, AND IF YOU HAVE THE CONVICTION TO CARRY IT OFF, THEN THAT'S FINE."

part is that because of my platform, I can try out new things. I can perform my own songs and release music. I've got an album on the way."

As sarcastic as she likes to be, Sum Ting never seems ungrateful for her swathes of support. In fact, she appears to be on cloud nine, happy to ride her recent waves of success and afraid to analyze the situation lest she jinx it. "I don't care about anything!" she declares. "The only thing I care about is the people I love most, and that's the only thing that got a rise out of me on *Drag Race*. The day I went home, everything fell together perfectly. I was eliminated and I went home to Reading. The next day, my partner and I went to an orchard, and it was cherry blossom season and there was blossom raining on us out of the sky like confetti. Life is so strange."

"A few months later, I was flogging [selling] T-shirts at Drag Con with my face on," she exclaims. "If a year ago you had told me that most of my profits came from flogging T-shirts with my face on, I'd tell you you were a liar. I feel like I just sit on this magical train and it just goes from stop to stop to stop and I say, 'Okay then!'"

So what, if anything, could ruffle her feather boa? "If I get to a gig and the sound system doesn't work, then it's over," she snaps. "That's the only thing in the world that I ask for. I'm not Mariah. I'm not a diva. I don't need bottles of champagne, roses, or red M&Ms. As a singer, I just need a sound system with a monitor on stage and some decent reverb. That's all any singer needs."

"Although, when I was touring the UK, doing gig after gig after gig, Divina Di Campo decided it would be a lovely idea to give me her flu. *Thanks bitch!* So I got the Divina flu and completely lost my voice. As a live performer, I didn't have a lip-sync track or a backup number, so on the final night of the UK tour, I had to get the audience to sing most of my lyrics. I barely scraped through. That was the worst thing that has ever happened to me. But the world didn't end. I'm still here."

Sum Ting was famously not out to her parents, as a drag queen or even as a gay man, before hitting the big time. *Drag Race* left her no choice but to let the cat out of the bag. "They're sweet with it," she reveals. "They're actually really cool with it. When we filmed the show, I realized I had a short time limit between production and airing to tell my parents."

"I called my dad and said, 'Hey Dad! I'm bringing my boyfriend back this weekend for food,' and he said, 'Boyfriend? Do you mean girlfriend?' and I said, 'No, I mean boyfriend!' and hung up. Then I called my mom and said the same thing, and she just asked what food I wanted. I had to check she had heard me right, but she was really more concerned with dinner. So that was nice."

"I was prepared to go my whole life without introducing my parents to my partner or telling them anything about my life. That was a much better reaction than I had expected. We went back a second time at Christmas, after the show had aired, and they were arguing over their favorite drag queen."

So with so many goals checked off, where is the Sum Ting Wong express headed next? "I just want to be sat on a late night chat show doing the promo work like I'm Lady Gaga," she exclaims. "I just want to be sat in front of a live studio audience telling them to buy my album. That's all I want to do for a living."

She already has an outfit picked out for the big launch. "I'd be a twat about it and insist on using the cheapest material possible," she says. "They could offer an unlimited budget and I would make a dress out of used fast-food packaging. I would link up sauce sachets and just stink all the way down the red carpet. For Pride, I want to make a dress out of processed cheese slices. They might melt, but then it would just be like a moving dress that changes shape on my body throughout the day."

While fame hasn't changed Sum Ting much, she's keenly aware of her visibility, particularly with regard to a new generation of drag devotees. "I have to be more mindful because I have a fanbase," she acknowledges. "I know that I have quite a young fanbase as well, so I have a responsibility to them, not so much to be a role model—because if you're looking to me to be a role model, then you're clearly looking in the wrong place—but it is nice to know that I have some sort of effect on some people's lives."

"My advice to anyone wanting to dip their toe in the waters of drag is to really think about wigs," she instructs. "Hair is quite literally such a huge part of drag, and it's a skill that everybody neglects because you can outsource it, but then everyone ends up with the same hairstyles. I would suggest learning everything you can about hair and then get to work on an old wig. You can spend an hour on hair or you can spend 20 hours, but it's all in the finishing touches. Take your time, be patient with it, and get yourself a handheld steamer."

"Beyond that," she advises, "stop worrying. Just don't give a fuck. Do exactly what you're doing right now and just see where it takes you. Also, if you're going to steal from other queens, then start small with something like bobby pins or loose change so they're less likely to notice. And never, under any circumstances, get caught."

"Why use structured wool when you can use plastic blackout blinds to make an outfit? My two-piece suit created in two days on *Drag Race UK* for the sewing challenge."

60 SECONDS
WITH SUM TING

**DESCRIBE YOURSELF
IN THREE WORDS**

Very large lady.

**WHERE IS YOUR
SPIRITUAL HOME?**

New York.

**WHAT IS YOUR FAIL-SAFE
PARTY TRICK?**

I can stick phones to
my head.

**WHAT WOULD YOU NEVER
LEAVE THE HOUSE WITHOUT?**

Flip-flops.

**HOW DO YOU HANDLE
A CRISIS?**

Um … There's no time for
emotions, so I take the
attitude that we just have
to deal with what we need
to deal with.

**WHAT IS SOMETHING
NOT MANY PEOPLE
KNOW ABOUT YOU?**

I used to be a chef, so I'm
probably the best cook
you've ever met.

**IF YOU RULED THE WORLD
FOR A DAY, WHAT CHANGE
WOULD YOU MAKE?**

I'd redistribute wealth from
billionaires to the rest of the
population. No one needs
a billion pounds [dollars],
like honestly, no one needs
that. I'd also get rid of
racism, sexism, transphobia,
and homophobia, but
that's a lot more than
one change!

ON TOP OF THE WORLD WITH GING-ZILLA

Self-described "glamonster" Gingzilla is the creation of Sydney-born cabaret artist Ben Hudson. Towering at 7 ft in heels, with a bushy ginger beard that is almost as long as her legs and a booming baritone that fills the room and then some, she is the very definition of a walking contradiction. Having performed all over the world, appeared on reality television, and swept up at the Adelaide Fringe, Ginge is one red-hot glamazon to keep an eye on. Just remember, her eyes are up here!

"To start off with," declares Gingzilla, "I am an experience. Not to sound egotistical or narcissistic or anything, but my presence is a lot. I'm 7 ft, I've got a gigantic ginger beard and I've got flame-red hair, and I'm always wearing something incredibly slinky and sexy. Not to mention, I've got legs right up to my clacker, so it's quite a sight to be seen. People don't understand how big I am till they see me in person."

The kind of cabaret Gingzilla performs is light-years away from the stuffy broads of yesteryear. "Coming from Australia, my idea of drag was very narrow minded," she explains. "My experience of drag was very much centered around Kylie [Minogue] impersonators or very high-camp pantomime drag from the '80s and '90s, like that Aussie classic *Priscilla, Queen of the Desert*. I never really got to witness the expansiveness of drag until I moved to London."

London proved to be an eye-opening experience for Gingzilla. "I went out to legendary queer club night Sink the Pink and I visited The Glory and places like Savage Disco and the ShayShay Show, which happened in a disused warehouse," she recalls. "It was around this time that I discovered drag could be so much more. So much more political and creative, and be a bit more … fuck you!"

Gingzilla trained in musical theater and, like so many ingenues of the great drag renaissance of the 2000s and 2010s, she found her professional footing in drag via a series of happy and not-so-happy accidents. In 2016, she entered an amateur lip-syncing competition with no intention of taking it too seriously, as she already had plans to pull up stakes and transfer to the Middle East for a theater production.

"I started drag two weeks before I had to jet off to Dubai to do a musical season and, suffice to say, once I first put on that wig and those heels, the bug had bitten. I then took it all off again to go and do the most hideous production in Dubai and be totally repressed. I got in trouble because my shorts were too short and obviously I couldn't be gay anywhere. It was a very contrasting experience from the liberation I had felt weeks prior."

It was to be a short-lived containment, as the universe had bigger plans for Gingzilla. "I got fired from the job in Dubai," she confesses, "and the week I got fired, I got offered a job working at London's Cirque Le Soir as a full-time drag queen, and that was it!"

"From then on, I was thrust into the drag world by the universal powers of woo-woo! Every single time that I screwed up, got fired, lost my house, my whole life basically imploded and I got propelled into doing more drag."

"A queen for all seasons … Spiced pumpkin latte, anyone? Lap it up."

"My London job at Cirque Le Soir finished right before the Edinburgh Fringe Festival," she explains, "so I just packed up all my drag and went to Edinburgh and I flyered. Every day for four weeks, I would get up, get into full drag, and hand out flyers for friends' shows on the Royal Mile."

Serendipity drove Gingzilla into the world of drag, but it was her ineffable persona that propelled her onto the stage. "The response from the public was incredible … people wanted to know what show I was doing, and I wasn't doing one!" she exclaims. "That's when I decided to create a solo show. I met a producer there at the Edinburgh Festival who brought me over to the Adelaide Festival, and then that brought me back to Edinburgh the next year with two shows … it was a snowball effect."

"The Adelaide Fringe absolutely blew my mind," she recalls. "I created Glamonster vs. The World, a whole show around female gender roles, mashing up characters from 1950s monster movies like Godzilla, Swamp Monster, and King Kong. I only had six performances booked in the run, and then word of mouth hit really, really quickly … I started winning awards for the show—best cabaret and the award for innovation—and we extended to a full run."

Being back in her homeland also gave Gingzilla opportunities to network. However, her focus was on making artistic connections, and she found inspiration from a huge variety of upcoming talent. "I met so many people and I met so many producers," she explains. "Fringe festivals are a beautiful place to meet and network with people on a very creative level rather than purely on a business level. People are there to share ideas, and so it's all about, 'What are you doing? What are *you* doing?' rather than like, 'How do I sell you, kid?'"

Success in Australia at both the Adelaide and Perth Fringe Festivals led to two more successful sellout runs at the Edinburgh Fringe Festival in the following years, as well as gigs in the UK, Sweden, and Singapore, to name a few. Then in 2018, things went up a notch, and Gingzilla was introduced to an audience of millions when she appeared on *The X Factor UK* singing a simpering, slowed-down blues

"FRINGE FESTIVALS ARE A BEAUTIFUL PLACE TO MEET AND NETWORK WITH PEOPLE ON A VERY CREATIVE LEVEL RATHER THAN PURELY ON A BUSINESS LEVEL. PEOPLE ARE THERE TO SHARE IDEAS."

version of The White Stripes' "Seven Nation Army." Her triumphantly queer performance won unanimous praise from the live audience and celebrity judges, and singer Robbie Williams described himself as "deliciously confused" in response to Gingzilla's gender-bending glamour.

In 2019, Ginge took on another reality TV behemoth when she traveled to Los Angeles to appear in *America's Got Talent*, this time performing a rowdy, dynamic interpretation of Tom Jones' "She's A Lady," eliciting an uproarious standing ovation.

"I trained as a musical theater singer all my life," she explains, "and I have a very deep voice, which is kind of alluring-slash-bewildering for some people because they don't expect me to come out with a big baritone belt."

While TV appearances and awards propelled Gingzilla toward a substantial digital following, her heart still belongs to live performances, where she can get up close and personal. "I'm very much in your face," she exclaims. "A lot of my shtick is licking people's heads and making out with strangers."

Of her annual Edinburgh lip-sync revue, she reveals: "I like to create extravaganzas, so Late Night Lip Service is like a variety show, but it's also very performance art meets ridiculous high camp. I went to clown school, so a lot of my drag has influences from a mixture of places, from my clown training to my musical theater training, and I fuse those things together rather than offering traditional lip-syncing."

It's impossible to digest Gingzilla without addressing her striking appearance. The contrast of perfectly coiffed vintage waves and full facial hair makes her appear like an alluring but slightly unnerving combination of Rita Hayworth and Rasputin. "I was always intending to keep the beard subconsciously, because I like my face with facial hair," she admits. "I look like a pinhead without the beard. At the beginning of my career, I just had a small beard, and then I let it grow for a couple of months and people went mental because my beard was so extreme. It was a big, hefty, Ned Kelly bushranger beard. So I think it's just added to the magic of my aesthetic."

But what does all that facial hair mean? "I think, inherently, being in a heteronormative space is political," she muses. "Like our bodies are political. As soon as you put a lash or a lip on, or you blur the lines of gender in a heteronormative space, it's automatically political, whether you like to think of it or not. My beard is a political statement as well. The beard is really playing with people's minds, challenging what is considered beautiful, what is considered masculine. I'm subverting an attribute that is considered in many cultures to be the epitome of masculinity."

"My hair color choice is also very political … like a triumphant symbol of reclaiming the thing I got bullied for. Like all the things about me that I kind of put together in my aesthetic or I highlight within myself, whether it's my long legs or all the things I used to get picked on about, I kind of amplify them more and make them a political statement. I'm saying, 'Perhaps you didn't like this then, but you're sure as hell gonna like it now! Look how beautiful I am and how I've created this powerful image, and there's no denying that you can't keep your eyes off it!'"

When it comes to drag makeup, Gingzilla bucks the trend of many contemporary artists, eschewing hyper-stylized, over-the-top facial fantasies. "I think I go for a more natural aesthetic," she explains, "and it's obviously still drag, but it's a more realistic approach because I've found that the prettier I am, the bigger the effect of the beard and more masculine attributes, and the bigger the response from the audience."

"By far the hardest part for me was blocking my brows," she confesses. "I spent a year trying to glue them down and then I gave up and shaved them off. My advice is that's the easiest thing to do. Unless you have really big, bushy brows. I'm dying to see a bitch on the scene with huge, natural bushy brows. Full bush, like slugs!"

While her looks are dazzling, Gingzilla's ultimate tip for aspiring entertainers is to go beyond the aesthetic. "I feel like we are becoming so focused on what we look like rather than what we want to say or what we want to see," she laments. "I want performance, I want to see things that make me stand up in my seat rather than seeing another pretty bitch. I am over pretty bitches."

"I want to see thought-provoking innovation," she continues. "I want to see gender, I want to see style and grace. It's subversion, it's in your face, it's breathtaking, and it's fucking hilarious! Drag is simply the ability to express yourself and your gender in any way you want."

For Gingzilla, drag is like a magical window into interactions that would never take place elsewhere. "I'm allowed to do a whole lot more as Gingzilla. That beautiful outward layer of drag is really just a key to anything you want. I can sit in your lap, I can caress your face, and I can be intimate without knowing you. I can talk to you in a way that would be unacceptable in the street. I've done things in drag that I would be locked up for in real life!" she jokes.

"Ultimately, I want to bring joy into the world," she concludes. "That's my driving force. I just think of the silliest or most extravagant thing I can, and then I create it. I hope that if something brings me joy, then maybe it will bring other people joy. That's what I'm doing this for."

60 SECONDS WITH GINGZILLA

DESCRIBE YOURSELF IN THREE WORDS

Hilariously audacious GLAMONSTER.

WHERE IS YOUR SPIRITUAL HOME?

My seven feet of beautifully pasty, freckly skin.

WHAT IS YOUR FAIL-SAFE PARTY TRICK?

She don't need one, she's the LIFE of the party.

WHAT WOULD YOU NEVER LEAVE THE HOUSE WITHOUT?

A belly full of laughs and compliments for random strangers.

HOW DO YOU HANDLE A CRISIS?

Two ways: cool, calm, and collected/scream the house down.

WHAT IS SOMETHING NOT MANY PEOPLE KNOW ABOUT YOU?

I'm an open book. I'll tell ya everything about myself in the first five minutes of meeting. I can chat your face off.

IF YOU RULED THE WORLD FOR A DAY, WHAT CHANGE WOULD YOU MAKE?

Everyone gets a puppy! It's only a day, might as well have fun.

RAIDING A VILLAGE WITH

CHEDDAR GORGEOUS

Cheddar Gorgeous is a walking, talking work of art. She is a staple of the edgy Manchester scene and the legendary drag mother of The Family Gorgeous. Her approach to drag is radical, holistic, and playful, eschewing brand loyalty and step-by-step tutorials for creative chaos and delicious confusion. Climb aboard as she talks creative trespassing, hot glue, and transcending the mortal coil.

"The sailor was one of the first masculine archetypes that I explored through drag. Sailors are symbols of freedom, adventure, and liberal sexuality. It was inspired by a mix of Jean-Paul Gaultier, Tom of Finland, and Pierre et Gilles."

"Part of a collaboration with Fake Trash to raise awareness about factors contributing to climate change. Who would have thought desertification and soil health could be so glam!"

"I always think the first time I started doing drag was when I was a waiter," says Cheddar. "That wasn't because I was dressed up in silly clothes and put on wigs and makeup. That's because, as a waiter, you learn to project yourself into a room. I was able to use that as a way of getting away with things, as a way to break protocol and build relationships with customers."

While Cheddar has dressed up since her teens—a self-confessed geek who dyed her hair every color under the sun—she wasn't dressed in anything she would necessarily have identified as drag at the time. "So many people try to reduce drag to the first time you put on a wig, and in many ways, that reduces what we do to a kind of costume. I think that's really troubling, because, for me, the essence of drag is the art of the relationship."

Cheddar started consciously creating drag around 10 years ago. "I went through various stages of bloom," she admits. "You go through your early moments, which are very much about feeling one's way, much like one's first forays into the art of making love. You begin with a few fumbles and stumbles, and slowly you finesse your skills in the art form."

She originally chose the name "Cheddar Van Der Tramp" in 2010, after the *Desperate Housewives* character Bree Van Der Camp. "I used to look like a clown," she recalls, "and I would go out baking and handing out cookies. So it was a weird play on that person who thinks they're super classy and above their station when they're not really."

After that, Cheddar's aesthetic diverged from the twisted domestic goddess character and grew into something that was much more about her journey through gender and her insecurity as a man. "I don't know if I do identify as a man anymore," she wonders. "I don't think I identify as anything, but my drag started to bleed into the fears I had about my own attractiveness and a growing anger around gender. I stopped wearing wigs. I played with masculinity and I played with transcending species."

After several years researching an emotionally draining PhD on the issues of public sex and sex work and a brief stint living amidst the queer counterculture of San Francisco, Cheddar returned to Manchester and put the pedal to the metal with drag, this time with a new name. "I remember the day I changed my name," she exclaims. "It was Manchester Pride, and I was sailing with a group of friends. The fenced-off gay village was charging people entry, so we decided to raid it by canal barge. I remember turning to my friend that day and saying that I was going to change my name. She said, 'Don't change your name, I love it!' And I said, 'Wait for it. I'm going to change my name to … Cheddar Gorgeous,' and it was like a rechristening. That was the moment I realized drag was something I wanted to invest in, as my friends and I were staging a revolutionary riot and invading our own village."

"So there you have it," she concludes. "There's not one moment of birth because drag isn't a straightforward transition. Drag isn't about putting on the makeup. A lot like a PhD, drag is ultimately about you and about how you are able to be in the world. That doesn't start or end at any particular point in time."

While many drag queens are inspired by the hyper-glamorous divas of stage and screen, Cheddar's influences are more esoteric. She's more likely to draw from Athena or Cthulu than from Madonna or Marilyn Monroe. "I think drag ultimately is about being able to embody some of the fantasies we have of being powerful and beautiful or even ugly," she muses. "For many people, that might be emulating Beyoncé or a Hollywood screen siren, but I was never that interested in those things. When I was powerless, beings that I saw as powerful were the aliens, the gods, and the monsters. I think we are all trying to do the same thing, but I just don't think a lot of drag artists take it far enough. I get that Beyoncé is a goddess, but then why not just be a fucking goddess?"

When it comes to creating concepts for the stage, Cheddar's top tip is to cut things just a little bit short. "I think probably the first state is to operate at a level of bad time management and incompetence," she advises, "so that you have a great deal of restriction in getting things done, and that kind of acts as your impetus in order to make something happen. You have to be in a state of blind panic for anything truly beautiful to emerge. Sometimes the idea for a look will come from a theme or a story. Sometimes I'll just have a really lovely hat and want to create a look around that. The look informs the meaning of the performance. I have a unicorn look that I perform in a lot … that becomes the symbol and the anchor, and different stories develop from that."

"The unicorn is such an amazing animal," she elaborates, "because it's not masculine and it's not feminine. It's aggressive yet also soft. It's camp yet also ethereal. It's an image of sparkly beauty that's associated with children, but it's got a fucking weapon on its head. I think in some respects that is the perfect metaphor for drag, because we are these silly creatures that can be laughed at, but at the same time what we do is incredibly challenging to the world and challenging to what some people consider fundamentally unshakable about themselves."

When it comes to materials, Cheddar likes to improvise. "I like to use what falls into my lap," she confesses. "I'm a big fan of shopping at discount shops and hardware stores. A lot of the things I use tend to be quite industrial, so I use a lot of wire and glue a lot of things together. I'm not faithful to any makeup brands. I don't believe brands are particularly desirable or exciting things. I actually think they're a really horrible way to determine value in things."

In lieu of pricey consumer labels, Cheddar scavenges for materials anywhere she can find them. "The strangest material I've ever used is rust," she recalls. "I used bits of rust off the floor. I try to stick anything I can to my face to be honest. I've used metal, plastic, and wood. They're the most fun to use because they're things we're not meant to play with. I tend to think of makeup as a mixed-media art form rather than as painting. In 2013, I first did a look where I covered parts of my face in bark. I went into the woods in springtime and just collected all this bark and dried it out and created costume pieces and makeup with it. I remember somebody asking me, 'Oh my god, how did you get that incredible bark effect?' And I replied, 'It's bark!'"

While many artists may have a long checklist of expensive garments, accessories, and beauty treatments, Cheddar prefers to lead with a few key pieces and cheekily break some rules. "Some drag queens need to put on a lot of expensive things to look fabulous, and others just don't require that much," she jokes. "I say the same thing about lashes and nails. Some drag queens need that kind of extravagance. Others, we're naturally beautiful."

Cheddar cites Amanda Lepore as one of the most influential icons when it comes to glamour. "She barely wears anything," she ventures. "I wear these cups that are glued to my body to cover my genitalia, and then I put silver leaf and makeup all over my body so that the cup blends with my skin and jewelry, and then I stick gems all over my chest and face so it looks as if I'm made of crystal. If I was going to the Met Gala, I'd wear nothing but a pair of heels, silver leaf, and crystals."

Cheddar is famed for her supportive and inclusive approach to drag. The slogan of her Manchester drag family, a subversion of a quote from the film *Mean Girls*, is "You *can* sit with us!" Cheddar is also quick to offer help and advice to those who

"I THINK DRAG ULTIMATELY IS ABOUT BEING ABLE TO EMBODY SOME OF THE FANTASIES WE HAVE OF BEING POWERFUL AND BEAUTIFUL OR EVEN UGLY."

ask. "There are several things I say to young performers who are just getting into drag," she explains, "and the first is obviously, 'Run! Run! Turn back while you still can!' But the second is that drag really is a way that your dreams can come true. The catch is, they won't be the dreams you set out with. I think you need to be open in what you expect the world to deliver to you."

"It's also important to play," she stresses. "Don't think too hard about how you should look, or whether your makeup is good enough yet. Allow yourself to grow, because the best drag grows from real life. Don't let drag be your only thing, because we're approaching a dangerous moment in which people are starting drag and their only interest is drag. You end up with this incredibly insular art form that isn't really saying anything, and it takes the bite out of drag and makes it harder to engage with the world in an interesting way. We become servants of unregulated free-market economics. We lose our power and we become part of the very system that oppresses us. So have another life and another job. It makes your drag far more interesting, and it also makes your potential to survive much better."

Cheddar is not a fan of step-by-step guides as a way to learn makeup skills. "Tutorials can be useful for individual techniques," she volunteers, "like how to cover your brows or apply a shadow, but if you copy an entire tutorial, you're just learning to paint somebody else's face. I meet so many young drag queens and I don't remember them because they all have the same face. I don't really believe in makeup tutorials. I've done a couple in my time, and people are always asking for more, but I don't want to see a whole bunch of people looking like me. I especially don't want to see people doing it better than I do it!"

Cheddar concludes that she wishes for everyone's dreams to come true. "I want everybody to go on a journey of self-discovery," she gushes. "I'm that annoyingly sincere. I really do want dreams to come true, but I also want the world to be more interesting, because I have to live in it. I think that one of the greatest gifts you can give to people is confusion. Because it's only through conflict that you can really appreciate how you differ from other people. It's only by continuing to throw out question marks rather than exclamation marks that you are able to get anywhere close to a shared sense of answer. You cannot create a shared world with people if you don't understand how they're different from you, and so I quite like moments of confusion, interruption, and awkwardness. I'm not trying to confuse you. I'm inviting you to be confused with me."

"Who doesn't love a pink unicorn? The unicorn is one of my favorite animals. It's camp and defiant, masculine and feminine, fun and fierce! It's the perfect embodiment of fabulous and angry."

60 SECONDS
WITH CHEDDAR

**DESCRIBE YOURSELF
IN THREE WORDS**

Fabulous and angry.

**WHERE IS YOUR
SPIRITUAL HOME?**

San Francisco.

**WHAT IS YOUR FAIL-SAFE
PARTY TRICK?**

I can make a pretty
convincing hooter
[horn] noise.

**WHAT WOULD YOU NEVER
LEAVE THE HOUSE
WITHOUT?**

Hope.

**HOW DO YOU HANDLE
A CRISIS?**

I don't know that I do.

**WHAT IS SOMETHING
NOT MANY PEOPLE
KNOW ABOUT YOU?**

I am actually really funny,
I swear.

**IF YOU RULED THE WORLD
FOR A DAY, WHAT CHANGE
WOULD YOU MAKE?**

I would make it illegal to
own more money than
you can possibly spend.

WALKING TALL WITH

YUHUA HAMA SAKI

Yuhua Hamasaki is a bubbly, ebullient bundle of quick wits and joyful energy. Probably best known for her spell-binding, East Asian–influenced fashion designs and cartoon makeup, Yuhua is equally adept when it comes to dazzling live shows, greeting fans and sharing a message of equality and unity. Perhaps most impressively, she's navigated the catapulting effect of global exposure that comes from being a reality TV megastar while keeping two heels planted firmly and fiercely on the ground.

Top: "Part-time queen and part-time housewife."
Bottom: "Do you think this is enough red?"

"I grew up in China, where the mentality toward drag queens and other LGBTQ+ people is that they are mentally ill," says Yuhua, "so my impression of them was that they were scary and I was fearful of them."

As she got older, Yuhua began to recognize some of herself in the drag personas visible on a burgeoning Myspace. "I saw people playing with makeup, hair, and the way they dressed, and I saw how brave they were," she recalls. "When I was younger, I remember playing with shirts over my head, using them as wigs. I remember wearing my sister's dresses, playing with my mother's makeup, and putting on her heels. I felt that that was some form of drag as well. Not necessarily the drag that I do now, but it was still some sort of drag."

As a young child, Yuhua was able to experiment with her presentation pretty openly, often wearing her sister's dresses to go out. "In the neighborhood where I grew up in China, people would say that they didn't realize my family had a younger sister," she recalls. "People just thought I was playing around, but as I got older, it was more of a shameful thing, so I started doing it more in secret."

Yuhua relocated to the United States when she was 7 years old. "I moved to New York and grew up in Chinatown," she says. "I remember in high school, I was bored. I didn't fit in with the boys because they were playing sports and talking about girls, but I didn't fit in with the girls 100 percent either. Then, one night, one of my friends took me to a bar and we dressed up in drag. It was the only way we were able to get in, because we were using fake IDs, and so security would not be able to tell if we matched our photographs."

Being in a queer space for the first time was a revelation for Yuhua. "I felt free," she says. "I felt like I was finally able to express myself, and not because I wanted to drink or party. I just felt like I was finally around people who were similar to me. It wasn't like it is today. Go back 10 or 15 years and there weren't many queer spaces where I could feel like that, even in New York City, and so that was one of the first times I felt that I fit in."

Drag became a way for Yuhua to reclaim some of the years she had spent suppressing her real self. "Growing up and trying not to come out as LGBTQ+, I felt like it was better to keep a low profile," she explains. "I felt like if I was to really be myself, then people would know I was queer, so a lot of the time I would just stay quiet. As I did more drag, I found that I finally could be myself and have fun, but also get a paycheck out of it. I think at any point in your life, if you get the opportunity to do something you love and you're getting paid for it, then you're golden."

Yuhua remembers her debut well. "I was 19 years old and it was in Hell's Kitchen in West Manhattan, before Hell's Kitchen was super gay," she notes. "I performed Gwen Stefani's 'What You Waiting For?' The response was pretty positive, mostly because it was full of my friends. It was my 19th birthday event, but the club believed I was turning 20-something, and I never told them my exact age."

Yuhua believes that drag has to reflect who you are on the inside. "As a child, I watched a lot of Chinese soap operas where people dressed in traditional Asian clothes and I loved how glorified their costumes, makeup, and hair were," she recalls. "It was so grand and at the same time very costumey and very drag. In America, a lot of performers reference divas like Joan Crawford in *Mommie Dearest* and Dorothy from *The Wizard of Oz*. My divas were the stars of Chinese TV shows, and I think that really influenced my drag."

Yuhua's drag persona is always evolving, but she is always sarcastic, funny, and a combination of glamorous and flirtatious. "I guess the word would be glamourtatious!" she laughs. "I like to look like a cartoon version of my out-of-drag self. There is a very costumey drag aesthetic to my look. I like to be sexy, but nowadays I also like to play with gender bending a bit. I think that's what makes a great performer, because you should always be evolving and changing and experimenting with different types of drag."

Yuhua's signature face entails dramatic, cartoony eye makeup; overdrawn lips; and enormous, spiky lashes. "I play with a variety of eye looks, bright colors, and different shapes," she says. "I used to do a similar face every performance because I was always touring, but when I'm at home, I like to get creative and have fun being a little more experimental. I think showing the collarbone is so sexy. I usually wear my drag without a necklace with big earrings and the collarbone highlighted. I remember seeing supermodels in magazines where they're slouching and I think that's very sexy and glamorous, but also very innocent."

Sometimes Yuhua might get to a show and realize that she doesn't have all the makeup she would like, but she advises that it's fine to improvise. "If I'm missing an eyeshadow, I end up using my contour color," she reveals. "If I don't have the right color lipstick, I end up using eyeshadows. If I don't have my primer, I can use lotion. If I don't have highlight powder, I can use white eyeshadow. I think there are always ways to play with makeup."

When it comes to storing her drag, Yuhua lives in New York City, where every square inch of space counts. "I have my drag closet, which is 90 percent drag and

10 percent nondrag clothes," she laughs. "It's very cramped. I sleep right next to my drag and right next to my sewing machine. I make a lot of my own costumes because that saves me money, and then I can tailor garments to exactly the style I want without depending on other people."

Drag for Yuhua is anything you want it to be and anything that expresses how you feel on the inside. "There are no rules," she insists. "As long as you're having fun, then you are doing drag properly. If you're not having fun, then I think you need to find out who you really are and pull from that to show your true colors to the world. A lot of people don't realize this, but when you wake up in the morning and choose your outfit, you are already doing drag, because you are going into your heart and finding the colors and expressions that you want to show to the outside world. It's like RuPaul says, 'We're all born naked and the rest is drag.'"

Yuhua's life changed drastically when, in 2018, she was announced as a contestant on the 10th season of reality behemoth *RuPaul's Drag Race*. "Even auditioning changed my life, because the application process forces you to reflect on your strengths and weaknesses," she explains. "I'm very comfortable with myself, but at the same time we can always work to be a better version of ourselves."

With greater exposure comes increased scrutiny, but Yuhua doesn't let internet trolls get to her. "There are always going to be negative comments, but you have to realize that there are also plenty of positive comments, too," she reflects. "I've always had a thick skin because I was bullied as a kid. Usually, when you become a drag queen, you've phased that out already, but after *Drag Race*, there was not just one negative comment, but tens of thousands of negative comments, and you have to learn to ignore them. At first, it was challenging, because I was not used to it, but to use an analogy: If I'm walking down the street and somebody says something negative, I have to keep going because I have a place to get to. I cannot stop and focus my energy on a negative comment from a stranger because I have somewhere to be."

"WHEN YOU WAKE UP IN THE MORNING AND CHOOSE YOUR OUTFIT, YOU ARE ALREADY DOING DRAG, BECAUSE YOU ARE GOING INTO YOUR HEART AND FINDING THE COLORS AND EXPRESSIONS THAT YOU WANT TO SHOW TO THE OUTSIDE WORLD."

Yuhua tends to brush off ignorance and focus on more positive interactions. "I was at a show in Dallas at a meet and greet," Yuhua recalls, "and someone came up to me and said, 'I love you, I love you, I love you!' They bought a bunch of my merch and told me they loved how I spoke on my podcast, but that was before I had done a podcast. Then I realized, 'Damn, this person thinks I'm Gia Gunn!' I've been mistaken for Gia plenty of times, as well as Jujubee and Ongina. I find it hilarious!"

"It was frustrating that they couldn't tell us apart," she admits, "but at least the person made it up for it by buying a bunch of my merch!"

Drag presents its fair share of challenges when it comes to cultivating a personal life, especially with Yuhua's high profile. "I'm on dating apps," she reveals, "I don't even have a drag face on, but people will still message me quotes that I've said on *Drag Race* or a photo of me in drag and I find that so funny."

Drag has given Yuhua confidence, determination, and courage that make up for any challenges. "Yuhua Hamasaki is like a superhero," she says. "If you're confused by that, just picture yourself as a kid when you dressed up as Superman, Spiderman, or Catwoman. You feel empowered, and that's exactly what drag gives me."

When it comes to politics, Yuhua believes drag performers simply being themselves is enough of a statement. "When you're in drag, you are pushing the norm and doing everything society tells you not to do: being visibly queer and dressing in a gender you aren't meant to and saying things that most people are afraid to say," she argues. "When I'm in drag, I like to pull a lot of influence from my Asian culture, but also from the things I believe in, which are queer rights and human rights. I am standing up for these things in my art, whether it is in my costumes or my photos. Hopefully people can take a message away that although drag is campy, we also need equality and human rights. Also, if I can glorify my own culture and heritage, then they can embrace theirs, whether they are black, Muslim, Latinx, a woman, or an immigrant. If I can do it as a drag queen, they can have the freedom to be themselves no matter what."

Top: "Sometimes a queen has to be her own knight to get things done!"
Bottom: "This is not a fashion statement: I'm just cold."

60 SECONDS WITH YUHUA

DESCRIBE YOURSELF IN THREE WORDS

Sarcastic, funny, and bootleg!

WHERE IS YOUR SPIRITUAL HOME?

Wherever I feel comfortable, but location-wise, NYC.

WHAT IS YOUR FAIL-SAFE PARTY TRICK?

To pretend I'm drunk, even though I don't drink, so I can blame nonexistent alcohol.

WHAT WOULD YOU NEVER LEAVE THE HOUSE WITHOUT?

Keys; wallet; and, since I'm a 21st-century baby, my phone.

HOW DO YOU HANDLE A CRISIS?

Without stress and by thinking calmly.

WHAT IS SOMETHING NOT MANY PEOPLE KNOW ABOUT YOU?

I'm usually the first one in a group to get out of drag whenever a show is done.

IF YOU RULED THE WORLD FOR A DAY, WHAT CHANGE WOULD YOU MAKE?

Have working toilets in every household!

149

Rebels and

PUNK

Revolutionaries

Drag is raw, drag is dark, and drag is dangerous.
Alternative artists eschew the pomp of the pantomime and
explore new frontiers, from gothic horror to counterculture.
These pioneers challenge mainstream ideals of beauty and
antagonize the boundaries of gender. It's drag, bitch, but
not as we know it!

REDEFINING SEXY WITH
CHIYO

CHIYO is the self-described Dark Prinx of the UK drag circuit, a radical trailblazer and lovable rogue who isn't afraid to dance to the beat of his own drum. When he's not challenging mainstream stereotypes of drag or setting crowds alight with his fiercely politicized performances, CHIYO is also a producer and promoter, showcasing alternative bodies and stagecrafts in safe spaces created for the benefit of his community. Here, he explains why drag doesn't always have to be a laugh parade in a feather boa in order to deserve your attention.

"Taken for a feature called 'WOOF: Redefining Sexy,' a photoshoot with Corinne Cumming, originally featured in QX magazine."

"**D**rag is going on stage, owning yourself, and leaving," says CHIYO. "I don't really like to think of drag as just dressing up as this, that, or the other. I don't think what I do is male illusion. It's more of a feeling. It's a sense of empowerment. I wish that I could describe how I feel when I'm on stage and show that exact moment to give people a sense of what I do."

When asked what he does for a living, CHIYO doesn't feel that being a drag king elicits quite the same level of instant admiration afforded to queens in the current boom. "It's very bizarre, in this world of drag and gender-blurring, when your career is literally fucking up gender, that we still have this binary view of kings and queens," he reflects. "We're in a world where we are supposedly freeing ourselves from gender and yet there is still a definite social and financial disparity."

What CHIYO loves most about being a performer is the chance to be present in queer spaces, both around diverse performers and supportive audiences. "I love working in LGBTQ+ venues and being surrounded with people who are all part of the same community because of their sexuality, their gender, or both," he reveals. "That sense of community is what I enjoy the most and the reason I wouldn't want to be doing anything else."

CHIYO started drag three years ago. He entered a competition called Man Up, which is the largest drag king contest in Europe, and things took off quicker than a glitter cannon. "It was kind of weird, but I did a performance about mental health straight off the bat," he recalls. "I didn't see the point of me doing drag unless I was doing something with my time on stage."

Like many people, CHIYO got into drag by watching it on TV, and that's what opened his mind up to the art form. However, it was on TV that he also noticed the limitations of access for queer artists who did not fit an archetypal drag queen mold. "I was just seeing all these phenomenal queens who were so polished and in a way showing a completely different craft," he remembers. "I felt intimidated to go on stage and try this thing unless I was saying something important. There's only so many times performers can do the same lip-sync to Britney Spears, so for my first performance, I did a stage act about Borderline Personality Disorder. It was an amazing experience. Afterward, I was overwhelmed with euphoria. I got a standing ovation!"

The rise in drag's popularity has impacted performers like CHIYO in terms of opening up a lot of new opportunities, but problems can arise when diverse and alternative drag artists become dependent and reliant on drag queens and cis gay male allies to offer them a platform to join in. "The whole of drag is becoming more mainstream and more popular, but it's largely drag queens getting asked to host hen dos, brunches, and pride festivals," he explains. "A large proportion of the time, performers like me only make it onto those lineups and into those spaces if the person who was invited in the first place brings us along."

CHIYO is thankful to have many drag queen friends who recognize that other performers don't get the same kind of opportunities. Many of these performers have used their career breaks to redistribute the platform. "That's great if it helps drag kings, drag things, trans people, and people of color," he says. "However, there is still a problem if we have to become dependent on more privileged performers to keep platforming us. That's why it's so important that we also make our own spaces."

CHIYO produces a variety show called Woof, which is a platform designed to redefine what it means to be sexy. "When I was growing up, even though I was queer as fuck and even though I was looking at gay magazines, there were never bodies that truly reflected how I felt or anything that represented true queer diversity and visibility," he explains. "Even in the drag world, it's seen as something radical if a trans person gets up on the stage and talks about being trans. I wanted to create a space in which that was normal, so Woof is about platforming anyone who doesn't fit the cookie-cutter mold of sexy, basically anyone who isn't a skinny, able-bodied, white, cis man."

For several years, CHIYO has been a practitioner of open-chest binding, a technique that uses medical-grade plaster to flatten the chest outward and create a flat surface for a traditional male illusion. However, he has recently undergone top surgery, which has not only been a euphoric experience for him personally, but also a game-changer for getting into drag. "It's very strange now; I'm in this unknown territory where getting ready used to take me two and a half hours," he reflects, "but I've completely chopped two kilos [pounds] off my body, so I don't have to bind anymore and I'm adjusting to new processes. Now it takes me between an hour and an hour and a half."

When you say the word "drag," many people immediately conjure a mental image of a drag queen, and they're thinking first about styled wigs and false eyelashes. CHIYO wants to dispel the notion that kings cannot participate equally in the joys of glamour and camp. "I think because of the lack of parity in how men and women style themselves in the heteronormative world, people struggle to fathom that anyone who is doing a different sort of gender presentation to high-glamour femininity is still using just as much makeup," he says. "There's a common misconception that drag kings just stick on a false mustache, but many of us still wear wigs, we still use nails and accessories, and we still spend hours on our makeup."

Just like some drag queens, CHIYO shaves off the outer half of his eyebrows, because it aids in drawing new shapes and gives him the opportunity to do more with his facial expression. "Kings also need some kind of foundation, concealer, and contour palette to carve out a more masculine face," he reveals. "I draw a dark contour from the corner of my jaw to the chin in a straight line to square it off. Then I draw from the corner of my eyeliner to the center of the jaw to create a sharp, angular cheek bone. It's also great to have colored eyeshadow palettes. Just because you're a king does not mean you can't play around with color."

CHIYO's fashion sense pays homage to princely rogues and dandies—those vagabonds on the fringes of society aping the flair and flourish of the bourgeoisie. "My personal style is influenced by Prince and Michael Jackson," he reveals. "When you see their energy, they are so fluid in their mannerisms, their gender, and their iconic fashion moments. I also love Puss In Boots," he laughs. "Growing up, I always wanted to be a little Puss In Boots. I also love to use scraps of old things and trying to make them current. I'm not a fan of symmetry and I love the early Boy George look, lots of fringe detail, 1970s rock, and punk."

While many drag artists choose to lip-sync to a well-known song, more and more artists are choosing to create their own mashups and mixes, playing around with sound and even recording their own voices in order to perform original monologues within their acts. "You can include pop-culture references, themes, or even create your own entire narrative from sound," explains CHIYO. "A lot of people think drag is just lip-syncing to one track, but actually the possibilities are endless. You have more autonomy with a mix and more of a chance to build a story."

CHIYO warns against the perils of going overboard when creating musical mashups. The secret, he believes, is to edit yourself ruthlessly and make complementary selections. "If you're telling a story, don't make it too long, because

"THERE'S A COMMON MISCONCEPTION THAT DRAG KINGS JUST STICK ON A FALSE MUSTACHE, BUT MANY OF US STILL WEAR WIGS, WE STILL USE NAILS AND ACCESSORIES, AND WE STILL SPEND HOURS ON OUR MAKEUP."

you want to leave people wanting more," he advises. "It's important to practice making mixes until you feel just right, so do explore and enjoy that."

When it comes to political comparisons between kingery, the art of the drag king, and queenery, CHIYO has several thoughts. "The thing about drag kings is that we take something that is toxic, like hypermasculinity, misogyny, and the patriarchy, and we not only critique it, but then we also have fun with it and make it entertaining," he explains. "So while drag queens are taking something like femininity that the queer community already glorifies and sees as powerful and subversive, kings have to work with a gender presentation that is often seen as the enemy and then reinvent that. That in itself is a very hard thing to do."

The misconceptions around the art of kingery have sometimes led to a few ruffled feathers. "I have been booed once, but I see that as a success," CHIYO recalls. "Booing is just clapping from ghosts. I was working in a ratty old boozer filled with older men, and they had never seen a drag king perform before. I did a performance about mental health and they just started booing, but I refused to stop. I just carried on. Upon reflection, it was a lot to handle, but at the time I just didn't give a fuck."

"Drag is political. Full stop," CHIYO insists. "Anyone who says otherwise just has the privilege to turn a blind eye to the politics of certain bodies in public spaces. To say that drag isn't political, just because you don't talk about party politics in your work, is a massive invalidation of widespread queerphobia and of the vulnerable people and minorities within the drag community."

The biggest lesson CHIYO has learned from drag is queer solidarity and the importance of community. "I've become notorious for criticizing the ugly side of the scene and the inequality I've faced," he admits, "but ultimately I've worked incredibly hard to get to a point where being a drag artist is my sole profession, and I don't regret having to kick down a few doors to get there."

"Drag has also taught me confidence and assertiveness. People would probably be surprised by how introverted I am. In my own time, I prefer to be in my own space, listening to an audiobook or playing video games all day. When I get into drag, there's just a moment where something happens and you're just ready."

"WHEN I GET INTO DRAG, THERE'S JUST A MOMENT WHERE SOMETHING HAPPENS AND YOU'RE JUST READY."

60 SECONDS WITH CHIYO

DESCRIBE YOURSELF IN THREE WORDS

Resilient. Punk. Authentic.

WHERE IS YOUR SPIRITUAL HOME?

Any sushi restaurant. I love sushi so much! I could eat sushi all day, every day.

WHAT IS YOUR FAIL-SAFE PARTY TRICK?

Showing people my Instagram and hoping they find me cool enough to not ask me to do an actual party trick.

WHAT WOULD YOU NEVER LEAVE THE HOUSE WITHOUT?

Headphones. I will have a breakdown if I can't drown out the capitalist hum of the world with Lady Gaga.

HOW DO YOU HANDLE A CRISIS?

I cry, and then I tweet about it.

WHAT IS SOMETHING NOT MANY PEOPLE KNOW ABOUT YOU?

I cannot stand lasagna—it makes me immediately want to throw up.

IF YOU RULED THE WORLD FOR A DAY, WHAT CHANGE WOULD YOU MAKE?

All people in authority would be replaced immediately with black trans people.

CLOWNING AROUND WITH

EVAH DESTRUCTION

Evah Destruction is a macabre mistress of alternative drag and star of *The Boulet Brothers' Dragula*. Part glamour icon and part horror movie clown, her performances are known to shock and delight in equal measure. So roll up, roll up to the freakiest side show in town as Evah explains all about skipping rent, finding the light, and why you shouldn't fork out for your first batch of makeup.

Top: Alternative drag requires just as much polish as glam drag. Bottom: Drag can be dark, moody, and intense.

"**I** was about 18 when I started going to gay clubs legally," Evah confesses. "Before that, I used to sneak in. I saw my first drag performance at a circuit party, and it was Phoenix from the third season of *RuPaul's Drag Race*. To me, it transformed my notion of drag. Before then, I always thought it was just those heavyset, over-the-top, clownish men in Hamburger Mary's. Then Phoenix performed and I was suddenly like, 'Oh, so *that's* drag!' And it was gorgeous, and energetic, and it broke so many stereotypes. After that, I started watching *Drag Race* and supporting local shows."

It was at one of these shows that the young Evah first met a performer named Jasmine Antoinette, who would later become her drag mother. "She showed me a more theatrical side to drag," she recalls, "and that's when I started to realize that this was something I could take seriously. I was a musical theater baby and had been performing from a young age, but once I was out of school, I didn't really have a performance avenue, so I saw drag as a way to perform once a week while I worked full time, and it became a sort of addiction."

"I went from once a week to as many times as I could possibly get into drag," she admits. "I would skip paying my bills, I would skip paying my rent, all so I could afford to buy more drag. That led to many learned life lessons. I lost both my day jobs eventually, and then I spent five months on a best friend's couch, and drag became my full-time job forcibly! I was living in Atlanta, Georgia, and I just worked my ass off, sometimes for free, as much as I could, just to get my name out there and make myself known among all these glamazons and pageant queens."

Evah started out as an entertainer being "alternative, weird, and not afraid to get down and dirty." But eventually the scene made her conform to a more pretty and uniform standard. "I had to start performing more and more top 40 numbers," she recalls, "and look more 'passable,' to use that problematic word. So that transformed me into this local queen who would perform comedy numbers and look gorgeous."

"There was a lot of auditioning for *RuPaul's Drag Race*, and that was definitely a heavy part of my story behind the scenes," she admits. "A lot of people told me that I would be great for the show, and I believe I would be, but something just didn't click. I was auditioning from season 6 onward and I had to watch all my friends get cast, and that took a really heavy toll on me. I had to take a really hard look at myself and decide where I wanted my drag to go."

In 2018, Evah appeared on *America's Got Talent*, but the experience was not all she had hoped it would be. "I thought it was gonna be more than what actually happened," she explains, "but I was basically cast without having to audition, and it was a really great build-up. Then when it came around to the edit, I saw myself get vetoed by all four judges before I could even finish my set. It was still a highlight, because it was my first time in reality TV and I got to learn about the façade of reality television and how scripted everything really is."

In 2019, Evah was announced as a contestant on *The Boulet Brothers' Dragula*, which might be described as the haunted emo cousin of the longer-running *RuPaul's Drag Race*. She became one of the standout stars of the season, placing fifth and introducing the world to her deranged and delectable style of drag.

"*Dragula* was such an amazing, beautiful, traumatic experience," she remembers. "I owe a lot to The Boulet Brothers, because they took a chance on me, but also because *Dragula* is a community that resonates with me. The alternative drag scene just gets it. It gets political correctness and being more awake. It understands how to treat entertainers and to show people they are worth more than just looking 'fishy' or 'passable.' This community celebrates everyone who participates."

"For years, a lot of people were influenced by the glamour drag package that was sold to us, and then that became very mainstream and that's what people aspired to, because they wanted to be part of a movement. But now that we've broken down the wall, we're beginning to see that there's more than one style."

"Glamour and alternative drag are similar in the sense of polish," explains Evah, "because at the end of the day, you always need a little polish. That doesn't mean you need crisp, clean edges and rhinestoned costumes, but it does mean a fully realized look that has a clear message. You can tell if somebody purposely threw on trash and still made it look like a million bucks."

So what does she think about the rise in popularity of the darker side to drag? "I think queer people are very enticed by things that are anti-establishment, things that are taboo, things that are weird," she muses. "I think we just love the fact that it's darker over in alternative drag. That's why shows like *Dragula* are starting to pull bigger audiences. Younger kids who grew up on *Drag Race* are old enough to understand more, and they find it more interesting because they're seeing women, nonbinary, and gender-queer people being allowed to compete in a drag show. Not just men."

Evah's looks range from deranged pop starlet to gruesome and gory killer clowns and cinematic scare icons. "As soon as my makeup, heels, and wig are on, it feels like a suit of armor," she reveals. "I feel invincible, I can literally talk to anyone that I want without any sort of fear of repercussion, and it's a lot more fun. Out of drag, I have to be around people I'm comfortable with to open up. When I'm out of drag, I like to keep drag separate. I love to push it away. I've got to take personal time to take care of me, so I don't like to go out to the bar so much on my night off anymore."

As more diverse drag begins to permeate the mainstream, Evah believes it's high time to reconsider what many of us think the art form is essentially about. "Drag to me is inventing yourself a completely different character," she poses. "You're creating a character that's attached to you and who you are inside and just projecting that out, whether it be through dance, hair, makeup, costume. But it's also committing yourself to being that character and ultimately transforming and embodying that ultimate being that you yourself have created. I can't really say that drag is men dressing as women. At this point in time, it's ridiculous to even imply that, so what I will say is that you are embodying your ultimate form."

Beyond the dark and dazzling looks, Evah is an intense stage performer, famed for her haunting stares and the simmering energy of her stagecraft. "I like to throw a very mystical glance toward the audience," she explains, "and I always love looking straight into a spotlight because I feel like I'm looking at the entire room. It illuminates the face, and then you're very present. I always believe in thanking a person every time they tip you, squeezing their hand, giving them a quick peck on the cheek or a smile, acknowledging that exchange of energy."

"'Bad Romance' was the very first number I ever performed. I knew all the Lady Gaga choreography back to front and I remember I made $40 that night. It was my first ever drag performance, and, to this day, one of my proudest moments. I owe a lot of my career to Lady Gaga and her influence."

When it comes to style, Evah's approach is eclectic and frenetic. "I was diagnosed with ADD from a very young age," she reveals, "and it's manageable, but I find my mind is very scattered, so my drag relates directly to that. You never get the same shape for an extended period, because I always get bored of something I have in my

"I CAN'T REALLY SAY THAT DRAG IS MEN DRESSING AS WOMEN. AT THIS POINT IN TIME, IT'S RIDICULOUS TO EVEN IMPLY THAT, SO WHAT I WILL SAY IS THAT YOU ARE EMBODYING YOUR ULTIMATE FORM."

closet and I'll want something new. I'd say Lady Gaga and Disney villains consistently make up a lot of my influences, because I love big shapes and dark clothing, and leather and lace, and straps and long high-heeled boots."

"I usually like to give myself a two-hour window to get ready," says Evah. "It takes me about an hour and a half to get makeup on, and the rest can go on pretty quickly after that. The makeup I do at the moment I call 'fatigue, but make it fashion'! My mom and I share this thing where her eyes have gotten more sunken with age. I've inherited that, so my eyebags have gotten more prominent. There's only so much glitter and highlight powder you can use to cover up imperfections, so why not bring them out? I've started painting on a deep scoop under my eye, and that has helped me to feel more authentically Evah Destruction, and I love the way my name sounds attached to that face. I feel more on brand with my name, which is something that's striking, dangerous, and scary. I always wanted a name that would catch people's attention. I also like to add this element of being kind of werewolf-ish by showing off my body hair and making a bushy brow. I feel like it's sort of a character of mine that I've embraced now that I've gotten more comfortable in my skin over the years."

Evah advises against pairing outfits with specific performances. "I never want a completed drag look to be exclusive to one track," she insists, "because then you fall into the trap of character mixes where you just have to perform that one number over and over. I usually prefer to find a shoe or a piece of hair and base the outfit around that. I like drapey shapes that create a lot of swish when you spin and billow out behind you when you walk. I do like feeling feminine in drag, even though I look like a bushy man, because I feel like it's destroying that construct between male and female and I love playing with gender."

On her dream ensemble, Evah says, "I would love Bob Mackie to design me the most enormous, quintessential Belle-shaped ballgown. I would take up the entire staircase. I always knew I wanted Bob Mackie to make me something, because he's dressed the stars, but he's also dressed a lot of more theatrical costumes. I feel like he could achieve that couture, over-the-top, mistress of darkness ballgown that would take up half the room."

And Evah's number one tip for new performers? "Don't spend $200 on your first batch of makeup," she warns. "Use your resources; talk to friends before you dive in headfirst. Pay your bills, pay your rent, and take every bit of advice with a grain of salt. Don't take everything so seriously. I think that's the best advice I can give. Oh, and take a dance class," she adds. "Then take another dance class."

60 SECONDS WITH EVAH

DESCRIBE YOURSELF IN THREE WORDS

Nerdy. Magnetic. Deadly.

WHERE IS YOUR SPIRITUAL HOME?

My island on Animal Crossing.

WHAT IS YOUR FAIL-SAFE PARTY TRICK?

I can make my eyes vibrate!

WHAT WOULD YOU NEVER LEAVE THE HOUSE WITHOUT?

I never leave the house without a cap on.

HOW DO YOU HANDLE A CRISIS?

I try to always look at the glass being half-full instead of half-empty.

WHAT IS SOMETHING NOT MANY PEOPLE KNOW ABOUT YOU?

I'm a member of the furry community.

IF YOU RULED THE WORLD FOR A DAY, WHAT CHANGE WOULD YOU MAKE?

I'd remove a lot of people's conservative ideologies so we can be a more open-minded society. I feel like that's where a lot of hatred stems from.

ANDRO GIN

Andro Gin is an illustrated menace, combining the hijinks of a Dickensian urchin with the debonair confidence of a comic-book villain. He defies expectations of masculinity, appearing in foppish and feminine styles, and has ascended to the rank of legend for his villainous makeup designs. Here, we talk to Andro about pirates, gender expression, and why mistakes are just an opportunity for improvisation.

Two very modern interpretations of commedia dell'arte masks that would allow actors to embody an emotion without the use of their facial expressions.

"I've been cross-dressing since I was a child," Andro reveals. "I was professionally appearing at birthday parties as Jack Sparrow. I was walking up and down tourist malls in full geish [drag makeup] collecting tips from people, and that's drag. I always say this, but I don't feel like you find drag; I feel like drag finds you. I grew up wondering why I couldn't play Sweeney Todd or Emcee in *Cabaret*. I went to theater school, and as much as I loved the female roles, I was more drawn to bad guys and antiheroes, and I couldn't understand why I wasn't allowed to be cast for these roles."

Andro Gin sees himself as a cartoon villain on the rise toward notoriety. "He's constantly at the 'defying gravity' moment in his character arc," he explains. "He's constantly trying to prove himself, trying to play the cops and make the princess's life impossible. He's an animated villain who is very queer, very gender nonconforming. If I had to define him, I'd say he is nonbinary and you can't tell what's in his pants, and that doesn't matter. He's just a miserable person who wants to make everyone else's lives miserable while looking pretty."

Throughout cartoon history, especially in the movies of Disney, villains from Jafar to Hades have been heavily queer-coded. "If you look at characters like Scar in *The Lion King* and other characters throughout the history of Hollywood," says Andro, "the bad guys were always a little femme and always had a limp wrist. They thought if they made the bad guys gay, then people would hate gay people. But then all of a sudden, queer people decided that Maleficent was ours now, and Scar was ours now. Instead of hating these characters, I was drawn to them in ways I didn't even understand as a young queer person, because they were coded to be us."

Andro has an extensive theatrical background and is very influenced by the Italian tradition of commedia dell'arte. "Italian farce is very much based in ballet-esque poses and overly dramatic physical comedy and characters like jesters and harlequins," he explains. "I also pull from mask work, because that requires you to really embody an emotion and a narrative without the use of your face. That may sound counterintuitive for lip-syncing, but that's where a lot of the persona and physicality for Andro comes from."

Andro operates like a fully realized and separate person with his own quirks. "I refer to Andro in the third person, but he very much exists in my head like another personality," he divulges. "I could be shopping and see a dress I think is hideously ugly, but then I look again and realize that Andro wants the dress. So I know this sounds like I should be diagnosed with some sort of disorder, but I listen to him."

It was through drag that Andro discovered he was nonbinary. "I should have known sooner, because apparently everyone in the world knew before me," he laughs. "When I came out as nonbinary, everyone was confused that I wasn't out already, and I was just like, 'No! I had no idea!'"

"What was strange for some people but very natural for me was that I was a drag king, which as an art form has its own history, but my male persona was highly feminine, and that gave me my own way of exploring femininity. I exist somewhere between a masculine woman and a feminine dude, and that's where my nonbinary ass comes from, and I have no one to thank but Andro for helping me to discover my relationship with gender."

When it comes to his iconic makeup looks, Andro is a master of improvisation, and his paints can take anywhere from one hour to four. "I can whip out a mug in an hour if I have to," he admits. "I don't like to because I'm a perfectionist and I like to leave the house pristine. If I'm doing a portfolio look or something for Instagram, where it's purely visual and not for a performance, I like to take my time, and that can take up to four hours."

People ask Andro about makeup all the time, because it's very much a focal point in his art. "I always tell people that I just do what I like," he confesses. "I just start smashing things on my face. I never had a drag dad or a drag mom, and nobody ever taught me. I don't necessarily have any secrets, but you don't need expensive shit to do a good job. All my brushes come from the local paint store. It's fine to invest in a good fluffy makeup brush for blending powders, but for the rest, I use paintbrushes that come in packs of 20 for $5."

Andro always starts with cream color and sets that with powder before applying accents with liquid color. "When it comes to mixing colors, I have a basic rainbow palette, but it doesn't offer much in the way of variety," he admits. "I tend to scrape off some pigment from the palette and mix it in a cup. If I want more of a reddish orange or orangey red, then I will blend to create those shades. Yellows are my favorite. I have a really pretty neon pink that I use a lot, and people always comment on the color blending and range of shades, but all I'm actually doing is using my yellow to blend that pink out to death, and then I get a whole rainbow of pink, fuchsia, peach, orange, and yellow. You don't need a million colors to achieve that."

Andro attended theater school, which he describes as one of the hardest and most traumatic things he's done, but he credits it with equipping him with a comprehensive toolkit for drag. "You always want to enter a stage like you've arrived from somewhere else," he says. "We had a six- or seven-step process at theater school where you had to ask yourself what your character's favorite color was, whether it was raining outside, what it smells like, all these things that inform your performance. That attitude just colors the number a little more fully."

A live Andro Gin show is likely to be a chaotic storytelling experience. "Because I'm also a playwright, a lot of my mixes come from a narrative standpoint, so you can always expect some type of story," he explains. "I always have an intro on my numbers where I'm not on stage and I'm coloring the scene. I do a version of 'Don't Rain on my Parade' as the Wicked Witch of the West. The audience hears her theme from *The Wizard of Oz*, and then I come out and terrorize them before going into the main number. That way they understand it's not Barbra on stage, it's this crazy bitch on the rise!"

Despite his extensive theatrical chops, Andro is no stranger to stage fright. "I get nervous waking up," he admits. "I have an anxiety disorder, so nerves are my life. I'm a perfectionist, so in my head, it needs to be perfect or else I'm a failure. When people see me before a number, they know not to go near me, and not because I'm a monster, but because I need time to center myself. I always find a quiet spot in the club or bar and I don't talk to anybody for about 10 minutes before I go on stage and take time to focus on the song and the character."

Theater teaches that there are no accidents, only opportunities for improvisation, and this is a mantra Andro applies to drag as well. "I performed a number at Wigwood festival in Miami," he remembers. "It was 'I Have Nothing' by Whitney Houston. At the high point in the song, I was to whip out these silk fans and have a dramatic moment, but I didn't realize the fans were in the wrong hands, so they didn't release and my dramatic number turned into a comedy number very fast. I was going up to people in the audience during the whole chorus I was supposed to be fan dancing, asking them to help me with my fans. Everyone loved the number. I cried afterward, but everyone told me it was very funny. So I always tell people things don't really go wrong, it's just about what you make of it."

Drag kings have been around since the late 1800s but still miss out on the kind of mainstream attention currently afforded to queens. "There is a very lush history

"I ALWAYS TELL PEOPLE THINGS DON'T REALLY GO WRONG, IT'S JUST ABOUT WHAT YOU MAKE OF IT."

of AFAB people, trans women, trans men, and every gender in the queer diaspora participating in drag," explains Andro. "So it is a little frustrating when those at the top with the responsibility to properly teach cisgender heterosexual people about our culture ignore that diversity to put money in their own pockets. Morally and ethically, that is not how I would treat that kind of power."

Thankfully, nobody has ever had the nerve to approach Andro with anything but positive feedback. "Sometimes people don't really get what's going on," he says, "but they love it anyway, even the straight men. Straight men have been some of the nicest, because I look like a video game character and they love that and will tell me I look badass."

The one thing that bothers Andro is tokenism. "I'll get people who don't like drag kings but want one king in their show, or a makeup brand who want one king to make up the mix," he shrugs. "I would rather just be seen as a great artist instead of being put in a box because somebody wants to fill a quota and seem woke."

"Sometimes I wonder if I were a cis man with my talent and accolades and everything I've accomplished, how much further along I would be," he muses. "But you can't focus on what's not the reality, so I keep trucking along. I do get frustrated with the misconceptions that televised drag has brought, but that's not my problem. Being on a TV competition is not where I see my drag going. I want to act in movies; I want to be in a history book. I feel like through drag you can do so much. There are one-person solo shows; there's vaudeville."

People are often scared to do drag because they worry about not being good, but Andro believes that not being great is an important part of drag. "You've got to start somewhere, and you're not meant to be perfect from the moment you start," he insists. "Drag doesn't have to be perfect. When you see queens on TV in these amazing looks, they haven't made them all. They are given many of them as rentals and they're thousand-dollar items. Drag never needs to be crazy expensive. The whole point is to have fun, feel cool, express gender theatrically, and be yourself."

The sagest piece of advice our dastardly antihero can offer is to know your worth. "Bianca Del Rio will say that you should say yes to every gig, and to an extent I think you should take as many gigs as you can," he advises. "However, there are people who will take advantage of you no matter how great you are. There are gigs I've taken for free, and I look back and I know better now. I didn't realize I could ask for money, but you totally can. More often than not, if people really want you there, they will agree, so my top tip is to know what your art is worth and what your time is worth."

Andro favors neon pink and yellow paints that he blends to death to create a rainbow of hues.

60 SECONDS WITH ANDRO

DESCRIBE YOURSELF IN THREE WORDS

Passionate. Fop. Menace.

WHERE IS YOUR SPIRITUAL HOME?

Listening to Beethoven and drinking warm coffee.

WHAT IS YOUR FAIL-SAFE PARTY TRICK?

A funny story.

WHAT WOULD YOU NEVER LEAVE THE HOUSE WITHOUT?

My crystal jewelry. My belief in metaphysical rocks gets me through my day.

HOW DO YOU HANDLE A CRISIS?

I don't. Not very well, at least.

WHAT IS SOMETHING NOT MANY PEOPLE KNOW ABOUT YOU?

I'm extremely spiritual.

IF YOU RULED THE WORLD FOR A DAY, WHAT CHANGE WOULD YOU MAKE?

I wouldn't want to rule the world, if I'm honest. I would divert my power to a council and have everyone discuss ideas.

MAJIC DYKE

Majic Dyke is the king of beard and titties, a nonbinary master of gender fuckery and smooth moves that would make a harlot blush. His slick boylesque routines and striking gender-defiant looks have brought him acclaim and popularity in the US and beyond. Here, he talks about cutting a music mix, creating realistic facial hair, and how to perform the perfect striptease.

Majic in cargo pants, boots, and an easy-to-rip-off jacket during a boylesque routine.

Top: The king of beard and titties looking regal.
Bottom: Majic will charm you with a love song, and then look you dead in the eyes. Irresistible charisma.

"I came to the US when I was 10 years old," says Majic. "I grew up in Nairobi, Kenya. Growing up as an African queer immigrant, there's a lot that gets suppressed culturally, so I was looking for a way to step into the world with my bold, bright colors, and drag was a door to a whole new world of expression, whether that be gender or sexuality. It was a completely immersive experience of gender euphoria."

"The way that I describe gender euphoria is that when I'm performing in drag and people are cheering me on, and I'm living my best life, I'm embracing all the things that I grew up hating about myself," he explains. "The fact that this is what is now being celebrated—that is when the euphoria comes in. My tagline is 'the king of beard and titties,' so my type of drag is gender fuckery, and I get to live my best life being weird, different, and odd. People see that and they're like, this is what we like about you, the fact that you're you."

Majic is named after one of his all-time favorite movies, *Magic Mike*, and his drag persona is modeled after its male lead; Majic Dyke is a male stripper who is super macho, sexy, and alluring.

"Growing up, I had short hair and I was assigned female at birth, so everybody just assumed I was a lesbian," he reveals. "I currently identify as pansexual and nonbinary, but at the time I thought, if I look like a lesbian, talk like a lesbian, dress like a lesbian, I guess I'm a dyke. I never took offense to it, because in the generation I grew up, it wasn't used as a derogatory term when placed on me. I know that in the past that word was used to cause harm, but just like the word queer, it's a reclamation of a word that was once used to tear people down. Now we use it as a way to uplift and celebrate our own identities."

Majic's first gig was a brunch show in 2017. "I didn't know how to put on a beard, so I had the people around me painting my face and helping me with my eyebrows," he remembers. "I had zero makeup skills. But once I got in drag and the music started playing, it was like every single ounce of anxiety I had, every bit of shyness I had, flew away. In that moment, I completely fell in love with the performance scene."

Majic took to the drag circuit like a duck to water. "Majic is essentially your favorite fuckboy. He likes to charm you, make you feel like you're the most special person in the world. When I'm performing, I like to channel the energy of my sexuality and the big dick energy that all male strippers have when they're on stage. Majic is the character who will play a love song and then come up and look at you dead in the eyes. I very much enjoy charming the pants off any and everyone."

"When I first started performing, I thought of Majic as a totally different character, because I was so shy and reserved in real life, and then on stage I would transform into this super confident, macho person. But over time, I started to really embody the qualities Majic had on stage, so now when I step out on stage, I see it as a heightened version of myself."

When Majic first started drag, he was predominantly performing in king-only spaces or the odd burlesque variety show that had one or two king spots. "Now that the drag scene is trying its best to become more inclusive, there are a lot more people reaching out to create a diverse array of artists on one platform without making it seem like they're having just that one kind," he explains. "Nobody likes to be the token anything, so I find myself in more places that are diverse and have representation from every gender, demographic, and performance style."

Majic describes a few of the basic subcategories within the art of kingery. "We have pageant kings, the bedazzled guys who like looking very polished," he begins. "There are celebrity impressionists and comedy kings, who do wild things to make the audience laugh. You've got spooky kings, vampires and demon daddies, and then you have alternative kings. I would consider myself an alt king, because I don't really fit in a box as far as gender presentation goes. I'm not trying to be a male illusionist; I'm just creating art that makes me feel good."

Despite advances made by kings in recent years, Majic is still keenly aware of the lack of representation at the top tier. "I strongly believe that kings need the same chances," he stresses, "but they don't even have that option to compete, and that's really fucked up. I think Landon Cider winning *Dragula* was eye-opening to some people who kind of ignored drag kings. Hopefully we see more opportunity for kings to be a part of the larger drag Olympics in the near future."

Majic's style is part streetwise casualwear, part dapper formalwear. "I grew up listening to a lot of male R&B artists like Usher and Ne-Yo, and they heavily influence the way I dress and style myself," he reveals. "Sometimes I wear suits and sometimes I wear clothes I can easily take off. If I'm stripping, I don't want to come on wearing 20 layers of clothing. Sometimes I just wear a tank top, cargo pants, and boots. Stuff I can easily tear off and toss aside when I want to be nasty."

Majic believes the secret to boylesque is taking your time and truly stepping into your confident energy. "If you're nervous, the crowd can easily tell that in your body language," he warns. "If you really want to be a successful artist, you have to fully own whatever it is you're doing. It sounds simple, but right before you go on stage, take 10 deep breaths and remind yourself that you are doing this for fun. No one is forcing you to step on stage. It's okay to be nervous, because you're about to step in front of a large audience, so remind yourself it's human to be nervous, but you're doing this for fun. Try to feel confident, and if you don't, fake it till you make it."

So what are Majic's pearls of wisdom for achieving a sultry and seductive male striptease? "Practice taking things off at home so you can see the timing and how it flows with the music," he instructs. "That way, by the time you hit the stage, you're not doing it for the first time. Nothing sucks more than a pair of pants that just won't unzip, and then you miss all your cues. Although don't get too caught up about each and every moment and get stuck in your head. Feel the music flow, and if you do miss your cue, it's fine to improvise. Nobody is going to know it went wrong, as long as you're having fun."

His number one rule: "Do not, under any circumstances, touch anyone without consent," he stresses. "Do not pull anyone up on stage without asking first. Some audience members really don't like attention being on them, and they just want to watch. As a rookie, sometimes you may get excited and want to grind on someone and they really don't like it, so always ask for consent before involving the audience."

Majic is one of many contemporary drag artists who perform mixes and mashups, audio design creations that layer different sound samples. "In the beginning, I would perform to one song, but I've learned how to make mixes throughout my drag journey, because producing audio mixes was a required skill to elevate my performance," he explains. "Both styles are fine, but with mixes I am able to tell more of a story by merging more than one song. Performing is storytelling, so you're learning how to create a storyline through music. When you create a mix, make sure it flows nicely. Listen to it and have a friend listen to it. Get as many ears as you can on it, because the last thing you want is a mix that doesn't make sense. If I went from a ballad to heavy metal to R&B all in one and that isn't intentional, it might leave the audience confused."

When it comes to cosmetics, Majic prefers to keep things simple. "I try to emulate the masculine face, so I don't do too many colors," he reveals. "I contour the cheeks

"NOTHING SUCKS MORE THAN A PAIR OF PANTS THAT JUST WON'T UNZIP, AND THEN YOU MISS ALL YOUR CUES."

and forehead. When I'm doing my face, I look at photos of male actors and try to copy the light and shadow on their face. The realism in the face creates a higher contrast with the rest of my look, because I do a really masculine face and beard and then I have a really soft body, because I'm still very feminine in how I like to express myself. I like the fact that I can combine both aspects of my nonbinary identity to create a contrast and have two personalities in one."

Majic's flawless facial hair designs are his signature feature and require careful attention to detail. "To apply my beards, I cut up hair extensions," he says. "I find hair that matches my natural hair texture, chop it up with scissors or clippers, and then I use Pros-Aide adhesive, which is a water-based medical grade glue used for makeup and applying things to the face. The first step is to put on the glue. After that, I take the cut hair and stick it on until I have the beard that I want. My face takes around an hour, and 30 minutes of that is the beard."

Being a king in a pop-cultural landscape dominated by queens comes with its pros and cons. "A lot of people assume kings are just male illusionists and that we aspire to look like regular male celebrities," he thinks. "If you look at people like Ed Sheeran, they're not embellished. They just wear jeans and a T-shirt. There's not much in the male world that rivals the Beyoncé diva look that people find entertaining. There are a lot of drag queens in giant wigs who are bedazzled head to toe, and people don't expect much of kings. There are a lot of misconceptions surrounding the fact that people don't understand the level of art that drag kings are capable of until they see them perform. A lot of kings focus on the message of their music and their art, so there's a lot of activism, a lot of sex appeal, and a lot of comedy. There is just as much entertainment in the king world as there is in the queen world."

Majic's advice to aspiring performers is to search high and low for clothes that fit well. "Drag kings often tend to wear oversized clothes because we're tiny," he laughs. "I would recommend finding outfits that make you look good and feel good. When it comes to makeup, don't be afraid to try new things. Don't be scared to be dramatic as hell or completely soft. Never grab anyone without their consent, and don't attempt any moves that you can't do on a normal day in your house. If you don't know how to backflip, then don't get on stage and try one just to impress the audience, because that's how you end up getting hurt."

60 SECONDS WITH MAJIC

DESCRIBE YOURSELF IN THREE WORDS

Sunshine. Ambitious. Empathetic.

WHERE IS YOUR SPIRITUAL HOME?

I'm nomadic, so I find peace in various people and places.

WHAT IS YOUR FAIL-SAFE PARTY TRICK?

Grinding on the floor Magic Mike-style.

WHAT WOULD YOU NEVER LEAVE THE HOUSE WITHOUT?

Chapstick.

HOW DO YOU HANDLE A CRISIS?

Remaining calm and being solution-oriented.

WHAT IS SOMETHING NOT MANY PEOPLE KNOW ABOUT YOU?

When I was younger, I had dreams of becoming a professional basketball player. But then I stopped growing.

IF YOU RULED THE WORLD FOR A DAY, WHAT CHANGE WOULD YOU MAKE?

I would abolish the police, redistribute wealth, and forgive everyone's student loans. Oh, and free healthcare.

INTO THE DARK WITH

MYNXIE

It is futile to resist the hypnotic glare of MYNXIE, high-camp cabaret queen, superstar DJ, club promoter, and professional goth. Her presence sits like a black widow at the intersection of alternative nightlife culture and frivolous theatrics. Originally destined for the West End, she was waylaid early on by esoteric interests and unapologetically climbed the ranks of London's queer underground, where she is now a recognizable fixture. So take your seats as the lights dim, smoke billows, and we meet the modern-day mistress of horror herself. Prepare to get spooked!

"A conceptual collaboration between Lotus Lasco and MYNXIE on the theme of poison, plant life, and possession."

"My first encounter with live drag was actually very queer," MYNXIE recalls. "I know a lot of people tend to experience drag in a very old-school sense in the first instance, but I was already involved in cabaret via the world of burlesque, so I was lucky enough to approach drag from the underground and see the variety of styles on display. Neo-drag was still very niche compared to what it is now, and it felt exciting and special to be experiencing the raw energy and politics of it all."

MYNXIE's first foray into the frenetic chaos of London's drag underground happened in the most unlikely of spaces. "My memory of the night is hazy," she admits, "but the earliest show I can recall was a queer revue in a random straight pub in Camden. There was a makeshift stage area marked out by sheets hung on string. I remember being incredibly drunk and watching a performer in a cheap wig and Christmas jumper [sweater] mime playing the pan pipes to 'All I Want For Christmas Is You' while handing out mince pies to the audience. I was confused, delighted, and conflicted. It was July."

MYNXIE grew up in the world of performing arts and graduated from drama school in Glasgow before moving to London. "I started auditioning for parts but found what was on offer very limited," she remembers. "I had always been fascinated by Weimar cabaret, queer punk culture, and B-movie aesthetics, but I hadn't really figured out a way to focus my career in that direction. When I realized how much underground cabaret was thriving in London, I suspected I might just be able to make a living from it. I decided to pack in the auditions and go my own way."

The name MYNXIE was already in the back of her mind, something she had used on teenage internet forums and doodled on school notebooks. "I think it's because my grandfather used to call me Minnie the Minx after Dennis the Menace's girlfriend, on account of my favorite red-and-black striped jumper [sweater]," she recollects. "I'd seen a picture of Kurt Cobain wearing one and thought I was being cool. I didn't feel cool after that, but the name stuck anyway."

To begin with, MYNXIE worked as a jazz singer, not least because she had a repertoire of songbook standards and a few evening gowns on hand. However, once she found her feet, she began to experiment with creative approaches to burlesque. "Burlesque was in the midst of its own renaissance," she explains, "although that was already becoming more commercialized and losing a lot of its satirical edge. At the same time, I was homing in on my own style and persona. The more I became my authentic self, the bigger my hair, outfits, and makeup became. Eventually, even burlesque became too restrictive and I naturally evolved into a ridiculously camp caricature, sort of like a Pokémon evolution, but with substantially more gin. Thus, I became a drag queen."

"The more I develop my style," she reveals, "the more I feel like I'm assuming my final form. Many performers develop an entire character for drag which is completely different to the person behind it, but I feel like my persona is incredibly authentic to who I am as a person. It just provides an opportunity to exaggerate all the bits I love about myself."

Stylistically, MYNXIE has one deadly stiletto planted firmly in darkness and the other in effervescent hyper-femininity. "It doesn't matter what the theme, character, or dress code is," she explains, "I will find a way to perform the hyper-femme goth version. My basic silhouettes for ballgowns and formalwear are drawn from classic B-movie horror mistresses and the femme fatale, with aspects of fetish. For more contemporary themes, I maintain that essence but throw in inspiration from pop culture, early '90s club kid fashion, and the leading ladies of grunge and punk rock."

MYNXIE is a contemporary face in a long and dishonorable lineage of gothic belles, nodding to the influence of Vampira; Morticia Addams; and, most notably, Elvira, Mistress of the Dark. "Elvira was referring to herself as a drag queen decades before drag was fashionable in the mainstream," she points out, "let alone before female drag queens were a visible presence. She's the perfect example of taking horror and darkness to such an extreme that you double back on yourself and become completely camp and ridiculous."

An acclaimed DJ and club promoter, MYNXIE considers music—and more importantly, the communities and fashions that surround it—as central to her inspirations. "I've always been a part of alternative music subcultures, and a lot of that was always inherently queer," she observes. "The blurred gender lines of emo, the heightened visual creativity of goth, and the raw political energy of punk are all things that seem to resonate with queer people and performers today. Even now, in my thirtieth mortal year, I am most comfortable in the middle of a Venn diagram between drag and goth, where queerness is a comfortable given, all bodies are encouraged to embrace creative self-expression, and you can experiment with dark and dangerous aesthetics in a supportive atmosphere. That, and I just really fucking love wearing black."

When it comes to makeup, her number one rule is to visualize the end goal, and then draw it 10 times bigger. "Paint your face so that a cartoonist could easily sketch an impression of you from memory," she advises. "That's drag makeup. You can use other faces for inspiration, but ultimately every person's features are very different, so you can only find your signature style through trial and error."

"A huge part of the energy I want to emit when I'm in drag is focused around the eyes," she explains. "The questions I ask myself are: if I were a dominatrix right now, could I strike fear and desire into the heart of my submissive with one look? And if I were an international spy on a deadly mission, would my eyeliner wings be sharp enough to slice an enemy in half?"

MYNXIE's key tip to achieving the silent assassin vibe is the illusion of ultra-precision. "Here's the thing: it's never *actually* that precise," she says. "When you're drawing huge shapes, they're absolutely never going to match or be perfect. The secret is making sure the edges are as smooth as possible and that the angles of your liner, shadow, crease, and brows all swoop upward in a way that extends your glare and complements the shape of your face. I tend to go over the edges of everything with a smooth eyeliner pen to make sure I get that fearless slickness. Your lashes absolutely have to be the right shape to complement the paint, too. I stack three pairs of varying sizes and shapes to frame the eye and add that hyper-feminine look."

MYNXIE's dream ensemble is something she's been considering for years now: a replica of camp icon Vampira's signature gown, as seen on *The Vampira Show*. "It would have to be screen-accurate in shape and cut," she insists, "but made from thick-gauge latex with black rhinestones melted into the surface. I would have a black, waved wig with the same black crystals dotted among the hair, an enormous black parasol, and oversized sunglasses. Naturally, I would arrive in a hearse and emerge in a cloud of dry ice. My train would be at least 20 meters [65 ft] long and continue to unravel from within the car as I made my entrance. Try upstaging that!"

MYNXIE uses a huge range of skills in her stage acts, from live vocals, to burlesque, to show-stopping fire-eating routines. "It's difficult to pick out a favorite performance," she confesses. "One that I always come back to is a burlesque act I created in 2015 for a punk freak show I was managing at the time. At nine minutes long, it was at least twice the length of your average striptease. It could have absolutely

"I ASK MYSELF ... IF I WERE AN INTERNATIONAL SPY ON A DEADLY MISSION, WOULD MY EYELINER WINGS BE SHARP ENOUGH TO SLICE AN ENEMY IN HALF?"

tanked, but somehow I managed to pull it off, and that moment really signified a stepping stone in my growth as a performer."

Drag enabled MYNXIE to blossom into a fully realized gothic chimera. "Drag to me is the creation and presentation of a fantasy," asserts MYNXIE, "often, but not always, used to explore and comment on gender. When I first started performing as a drag queen, I didn't encounter as much negativity toward my gender as I do today. It was actually other performers who encouraged me toward identifying as a drag queen, based on the draggy elements I was showing in my cabaret work, so it felt like a normal thing to do. My work was always going to focus on the feminine rather than the masculine, so I was always going to be a queen rather than a king."

In recent years, the explosion of pageant-style drag by male-presenting bodies in mainstream media has created a huge new audience for drag. "This is great in theory," ventures MYNXIE, "but if that audience isn't exposed to anything outside of that box, they may not ever see a female drag queen or understand that women have been doing drag for as long as it's existed. This has led to a lot of punters questioning the validity of what I do or even trying to tell me that I shouldn't be doing it."

MYNXIE is quick to point out that responsibility for some of these narrow interpretations falls to the tastemakers at the top. "The very famous host of a well-known reality television competition once made a comment about drag losing its edginess when women do it," she exclaims. "I find this completely bizarre."

"If the purpose of drag is to satirize gender, then what could be more punk rock than women parodying aspects of their femininity to an audience in spite of a society that mocks, shames, and harasses them for those exact things? Am I—a queer woman—not vastly qualified to pass artistic comment on my own gender? It's all a bit silly if you ask me. Gender shouldn't restrict anyone from any job or creative outlet."

Drag ultimately helped MYNXIE find her confidence and brush aside the reservations that held her back in day-to-day life. "Society has a tendency to chastise women for being too outspoken, and I always have that little voice in the back of my mind that wants to hold me back from being perceived as bossy. When I'm in drag, I absolutely couldn't give a single fuck."

"Drag in the mainstream is slowly becoming more diverse despite the odds," she concludes. "I think drag holds a lot of power for the very near future in terms of educating people on LGBTQ+ issues and politics at large. We already have drag queens running for office. Next, they're going to take over the world."

"MYNXIE, photographed by Damien Frost during WIMP, an underground club kid event. The theme was 'Funeral', and MYNXIE depicts a weeping widow"

60 SECONDS WITH MYNXIE

DESCRIBE YOURSELF IN THREE WORDS
Deadly. Camp. Vamp.

WHERE IS YOUR SPIRITUAL HOME?
Hell.

WHAT IS YOUR FAIL-SAFE PARTY TRICK?
I can make an entire bottle of prosecco disappear in just 20 minutes. C'est magique!

WHAT WOULD YOU NEVER LEAVE THE HOUSE WITHOUT?
Sunglasses. Regardless of the time of year.

HOW DO YOU HANDLE A CRISIS?
Stay calm and stare 'em down. Works every time.

WHAT IS SOMETHING NOT MANY PEOPLE KNOW ABOUT YOU?
I had a pink French manicure for a whole year of my life. I've recovered now, thankfully.

IF YOU RULED THE WORLD FOR A DAY, WHAT CHANGE WOULD YOU MAKE?
We'd be living in a fair and thriving matriarchy, that's for sure. And no goddamn kitten heels!

AUTHOR ACKNOWLEDGEMENTS

I'd like to begin by thanking my friend Crystal, who agreed to this project before any other names were attached and thus served as a seductive honeytrap with which to lure the other brilliant contributors.

Next I must thank Alice and Ellie, who supervised and edited this project, for being patient and supportive when I was tardy and chaotic. I could not have done half of this on my own. Thanks also to Steph at DK and to Max, Geoff and the design team for being great collaborators and having faith in my ideas.

I'd also like to extend thanks to Chuck SJ who hopped on board to help me with transcripts when 30+ hours of audio recordings overwhelmed me and digital software couldn't quite get to grips with the sheer amount of drag lingo in these interviews.

Finally, I am grateful to the numerous friends whose ears I chewed off while working on this book in near total isolation during the coronavirus pandemic of 2020: namely my parents, Jimmy Lavender, and the guy off Tinder I've been sexting throughout lockdown.

The publisher would like to thank the following for their kind permission to reproduce their photographs:
(Key: a-above; b-below/bottom; c-centre; f-far; l-left; r-right; t-top)

2 Felix Le Freak: Janet Cawthorne. **7 Monét X Change:** Steven Simione. **17 Felix Le Freak:** Elliot Moody. **21 Coco Peru:** Peter Palladino / Den Photography. **22 Coco Peru:** Peter Palladino / Den Photography (t). **27 Coco Peru:** Peter Palladino / Den Photography. **29 Adam All:** Emma Bailey. **30 Adam All:** Emma Bailey (t, b). **35 Adam All:** Emma Bailey (b). **37 Myra Dubois:** Holly Revell. **38 Myra Dubois:** Holly Revell: (t, b). **43 Myra Dubois:** Holly Revell. **45 Glamrou:** Lelia Scarfiotti. **46 Glamrou:** Alia Romagnoli /shado @shado.mag/make up by Rebecca Butterworth Magazine (t, b). **51 Glamrou:** Alia Romagnoli /shado @ shado.mag/make up by Rebecca Butterworth Magazine. **53 Peaches Christ:** David Ayllon. **54 Peaches Christ:** Jose A Guzman Colon. **56-57 Peaches Christ:** Jose A Guzman Colon. **60 Peaches Christ:** Ash Danielsen. **61 Peaches Christ:** Jose A Guzman Colon (t); Ash Danielsen (b). **65 Tasha Doughty:** @tashadoughty. **66 Owen Tozer:** (t, b). **69 Dan Goven. 72 Colin Smith. 73 Colin Smith:** (t, b). **75 Fay Ludes:** Jeremiah Corder. **76 Fay Ludes:** Guys and Queens (t, b). **81 Fay Ludes.** **83 Calypso Jeté Balmain:** David Franco. **84 Calypso Jeté Balmain:** Chang-Min Jonathan Hyon. **89 Calypso Jeté Balmain:** Chang-Min Jonathan Hyon. **91 Crystal:** Nik Pate. **92 Crystal:** Eivind Hansen (t, b). **95 Crystal:** Robbie Symonette (t, b). **98 Crystal:** Wolf James. **99 Crystal:** Wolf James. **101 Tynomi Banks:** Quinton Cruickshanks. **102 Tynomi Banks:** Jamo Best. **107 Tynomi Banks:** Jamo Best. **111 August:** Martin Schoeller. **112 Chris Bogard Photography:** (t, b). **117 Tracey Ahkee Photography. 119 Sum Ting Wong:** Elliot Moody. **121 Sum Ting Wong:** Elliot Moody. (t, b). **125 Sum Ting Wong. 127 Gingzilla:** Steve Ullathorne. **129 Gingzilla:** Aitor Santomé. **133 Gingzilla:** Henry Maynard. **135 Cheddar Gorgeous:** Ian Brooke. **136 Cheddar Gorgeous:** Fake Trash (t, b). **141 Cheddar Gorgeous:** Fake Trash **143 Yuhua Hamasaki:** Edited by Matante Alex. **144 Yuhua Hamasaki:** Edited by Matante Alex (t, b). **149 Yuhua Hamasaki:** Edited by Eric Magnusse (t), Edited by Matante Alex (b). **153 Chiyo:** Corinne Cummings. **154 Chiyo:** Bruce Wang. **159 Chiyo:** Oliver Reynolds. **161 Evah Destruction:** Toby. **162 Evah Destruction:** David Franco (t); Slevin Mors (b). **167 Evah Destruction:** David Franco (t, b). **169 Andro Gin. 170 Andro Gin:** (t, b). **175 Andro Gin. 177 Majic Dyke:** Sloetry Photography for The Cocoa Butter Club. **178 Majic Dyke:** Your Rouge Photography (t), (b). **183 Majic Dyke:** (t, b). **185 Lotus Lasco. 186 Corinne Cumming:** (t, b). **191 Damien Frost**

All other images © Dorling Kindersley
For further information see: **www.dkimages.com**

DK UK

Editors Alice Sambrook and Ellie Wils█
Senior Acquisitions Editor Stephanie █
Art Editor Geoff Borin
Managing Art Editor Christine Keil█
Production Editor David Almond
Senior Production Controller Stepha█
McConnell
Senior Jacket Designer Nicola Powli█
Jacket Editor Lucy Philpott
Art Director Maxine Pedliham
Publishing Director Mary-Clare Jerra█

First American Edition, 2020
Published in the United States by DK Publi█
1450 Broadway, Suite 801, New York, NY 1█
20 21 22 23 10 9 8 7 6 5 4 3 2 1

For the curious
www.dk.com

MIX
Paper from
responsible sources
FSC™ C018179